SPINNING UP SERVICENOW

IT SERVICE MANAGERS' GUIDE TO SUCCESSFUL USER ADOPTION

Gabriele Kahlout

Apress®

Spinning Up ServiceNow: IT Service Managers' Guide to Successful User Adoption

Gabriele Kahlout
Doha, Qatar

ISBN-13 (pbk): 978-1-4842-2570-7   ISBN-13 (electronic): 978-1-4842-2571-4
DOI 10.1007/978-1-4842-2571-4

Library of Congress Control Number: 2017935100

Managing Director: Welmoed Spahr
Editorial Director: Todd Green
Acquisitions Editor: Robert Hutchinson
Development Editor: Laura Berendson
Technical Reviewer: Göran Lundqvist
Coordinating Editor: Rita Fernando
Copy Editor: Larissa Shmailo
Compositor: SPi Global
Indexer: SPi Global
Cover image designed by Freepik

Distributed to the book trade worldwide by Springer Science+Business Media New York, 233 Spring Street, 6th Floor, New York, NY 10013. Phone 1-800-SPRINGER, fax (201) 348-4505, e-mail orders-ny@springer-sbm.com, or visit www.springeronline.com. Apress Media, LLC is a California LLC and the sole member (owner) is Springer Science + Business Media Finance Inc (SSBM Finance Inc). SSBM Finance Inc is a Delaware corporation.

For information on translations, please e-mail rights@apress.com, or visit http://www.apress.com/rights-permissions.

Apress titles may be purchased in bulk for academic, corporate, or promotional use. eBook versions and licenses are also available for most titles. For more information, reference our Print and eBook Bulk Sales web page at http://www.apress.com/bulk-sales.

Any source code or other supplementary material referenced by the author in this book is available to readers on GitHub via the book's product page, located at www.apress.com/9781484225707. For more detailed information, please visit http://www.apress.com/source-code.

Printed on acid-free paper

Apress Business: The Unbiased Source of Business Information

Apress business books provide essential information and practical advice, each written for practitioners by recognized experts. Busy managers and professionals in all areas of the business world—and at all levels of technical sophistication—look to our books for the actionable ideas and tools they need to solve problems, update and enhance their professional skills, make their work lives easier, and capitalize on opportunity.

Whatever the topic on the business spectrum—entrepreneurship, finance, sales, marketing, management, regulation, information technology, among others—Apress has been praised for providing the objective information and unbiased advice you need to excel in your daily work life. Our authors have no axes to grind; they understand they have one job only—to deliver up-to-date, accurate information simply, concisely, and with deep insight that addresses the real needs of our readers.

It is increasingly hard to find information—whether in the news media, on the Internet, and now all too often in books—that is even-handed and has your best interests at heart. We therefore hope that you enjoy this book, which has been carefully crafted to meet our standards of quality and unbiased coverage.

We are always interested in your feedback or ideas for new titles. Perhaps you'd even like to write a book yourself. Whatever the case, reach out to us at editorial@apress.com and an editor will respond swiftly. Incidentally, at the back of this book, you will find a list of useful related titles. Please visit us at www.apress.com to sign up for newsletters and discounts on future purchases.

The Apress Business Team

To my wife Jasmine for enduring the writing of this book.

Contents

About the Author

Gabriele Kahlout is the architect of ServiceNow at the Al Jazeera Media Network and in 2014 was recognized for outstanding achievements with the platform. Championing the transition to ServiceNow, Gabriele advises management, implements proposals, and confronts warts and wrinkles with users. Drawing on experience at start-ups and in innovative research centers, since 2012 Gabriele has brought to the revolutionary but corporate Al Jazeera his enthusiasm for change and a down-to-earth pragmatism. Gabriele attended the Freie Universität Bozen in Italy, the College of Charleston in the USA, and the University of Leeds in the UK.

About the Technical Reviewer

Göran Lundqvist is a technical consultant working for Symfoni ESM with a focus on ServiceNow.

He has a broad ITSM experience within both processes and technical areas, and brings over 15 years of knowledge in these areas. During these years he has worked as everything from first line support to third line support, team manager, process owner, and system administrator.

The last few years he has been in the ServiceNow field and is constantly looking for new things to learn about ServiceNow. He believes that sharing is the key to the future, which took him down the road to becoming a ServiceNow advocate, where he is an active community member and blog writer for ServiceNow.

Acknowledgments

First and foremost, thanks are due to Al Jazeera for giving me the opportunity to ride the ServiceNow wave in a corporate environment and for allowing me to share the insights acquired on the job with you. I had my first interview at Al Jazeera with Grant Franklin Totten, with whom I flew to New York a year later to launch ServiceNow at Al Jazeera America. Thank you for the trust that you have put in me.

Al Jazeera generally adopts a permissive knowledge-sharing policy, but our chief information officer Mohamed Abuagla has particularly encouraged us to be world-class in what we do and show it.

I could go on acknowledging many more colleagues at Al Jazeera, with Aamer Maqsood, Faisal Iqbal, and Imad Musa at the top of the list for facilitating the publication of this work.

Outside Al Jazeera, I thank peers in the ServiceNow community, some of who are quoted in this book, for openly and generously sharing with me their own examples and insights. Of all people, I single out Göran Lundqvist for technically reviewing this work.

My family and friends, thank you for enduring my seclusion as I worked on this book.

Finally, I thank the editing team at Apress for coming together to make this work the polished outcome that you now get, and for bearing with me through the creative process of writing. I kept on changing the table of contents, merging chapters and creating new ones. Thank you Robert Hutchinson for believing in the importance of this book from day one, Rita Fernando, and Laura Berendson.

Thank you all.

Introduction

When I joined Al Jazeera in 2012, the IT department was looking to improve the way it organized itself internally, and how it was perceived in the eyes of colleagues in this international media organization.

Al Jazeera has been at the center of the Arab Spring revolutions and its influence was being felt beyond the Middle East. Hillary Clinton called it a leader providing more "real news" than its American counterparts who she said were losing the "information war."

Inside Al Jazeera, it was easy to perceive the aura of pride felt in how Al Jazeera was challenging local and Western media establishments, and for IT this meant that internal stakeholders expected nothing less than world-class support and operations.

Analag satellite broadcast technology was extremely sharp and resilient, and as the WikiLeaks tweet below suggests, it was perceived as a core element of Al Jazeera's success. But with users' attention shifting to digital and the advent of Broadcast IT, expectations and dependence on IT were chaotically on the rise.

In this context, the IT department embarked on several transformational initiatives, one of which was the establishment of a Service Management function tasked to improve the processes through which the department handled its work, and the introduction of ServiceNow to aid in the transformation. So I was hired.

Figure 1. It's widely believed that Al Jazeera and its broadcast technology played a central role in the diffusion of revolutionary sentiment across the Arab world between 2008 and 2011

What occurred since 2012 and the writing of this book was not only special for me and Al Jazeera's digital transformation. The role that IT systems have been playing in our daily lives and in the corporate world has surged and, not coincidentally, so has ServiceNow's share price.

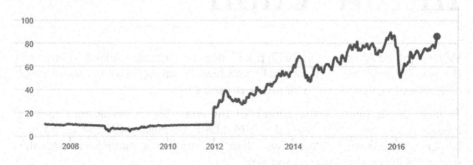

Figure 2. Share price of ServiceNow (NYSE: NOW) has been steadily increasing since its IPO in 2012

This is not to say that all investments in ITSM are rosy; you probably know from personal experience that it is not the case. In fact, numerous studies report on how commonly ITSM implementation projects fail to deliver on expectations, with failure rate estimates as high as 80%.

Despite false starts, ServiceNow achieved very wide adoption at Al Jazeera, and has contributed to a noticeable transformation in the way things get done here and in the relationship between IT and the wider organization. As testimony of this success, management was invited by ServiceNow to tell its story at the Knowledge14 ServiceNow conference, and I was named a Star of Al Jazeera Media Network in 2014.

In reality, credit for the transformation can only be partially attributed to the tool, best practice theories, or policy documents; the real transformation was actually in people.

As so many Service Management experts confirm: "To successfully implement ITIL is to confront human nature and succeed." (Denis Matte) This is what I want to share with you in this book: How to facilitate change in people's daily routines in an enterprise organization by focusing on visible returns on investment first, and staging drastic changes that typically sabotage users' adoption.

Who this book is for

Auspicious of great success for your ServiceNow implementation, this book is written for the benefit of application managers, Service Management program directors and fellow solution architects responsible for ServiceNow in their organization.

If you have already introduced ServiceNow at your organization or for a client but you are facing user resistance and not seeing the widespread adoption that was expected, you will particularly appreciate the pragmatic advice offered in this book.

This book is different from the typical pleas that justify a lack of progress with the need for heavy-handed executive support, massive ITIL brainwashing schemes, or hiring someone to consult for you.

In this book we acknowledge the people behavior challenge, but draw on insights from research in consumer behavior, web usability, and software engineering that worked at Al Jazeera. Examples will also be provided from other world-class organizations, such as Volkswagen, Berkeley and Harvard Universities, and CERN.

Three reasons to read this book

1. Your organization has invested (or is planning to) in ServiceNow licenses and implementation expenses. With a few bucks more, this book will help you get a better return on the investment and avoid falling prey to vendors.

2. You believe that the comprehensiveness of requirements, management buy-in, or ServiceNow's Out-Of-Box functionality will cause people to abandon their daily routines and jump on board en masse. This book may spare you disappointment!

3. You espouse the Agile methodology but seem to be at odds with the Waterfall arrogance of IT Service Management bureaucrats around you. You are not insane! This book will equip you with anecdotes to convince them or intervene in case they fail.

How this book is structured

The book is divided into three parts:

Part 1. ITSM in the Real World: Guiding principles and implementation strategy

Part 2. Essentials: Specific advice for the implementation phase of your project, with emphasis on email processing, on-boarding, and a front-end service portal

Part 3. After Go-live: Advice on managing development after Go-live, and dealing with scaling issues.

There are 12 chapters in this book, and at the end of each chapter is a list of concise and tweet-ready takeaways.

There also two appendices:

Appendix A: Provides checklists for assessing and monitoring customizations

Appendix B: Binds together bullet-point requirements from all chapters, for ease of reference

ITSM in the real world

Start by doing what's necessary; then do what's possible; and suddenly you are doing the impossible.

—Francis of Assisi

Despite all the hype, many IT service management initiatives are doomed. In Part I we look at what lessons can be learned, observe patterns in the success stories, and propose a strategy to maximize your chances of success.

Chapter 1: Pragmatic or tragic ITSM

Chapter 2: Innovators' ITSM strategy

Pragmatic or Tragic ITSM

Why ITSM initiatives fail and how to succeed

Decades of experience teach us that IT service management programs are really people-change initiatives, but that they are frequently mistaken for ITSM tool implementations or process documentation projects.

—Troy DuMoulin, Vice President of Research at Pink Elephant[1]

IT help desk teams have long been mesmerized by the advertised benefits of the latest ticketing system, showcased to bring order to the chaotic mess in IT departments and to vex relationships with colleagues calling for assistance.

This chapter describes the context in which many IT managers begin their IT service management (ITSM) and ServiceNow implementation projects, and the by now researched and documented critical mistakes many make in the process. Knowing how the problems manifests themselves, we then identify guiding principles to avoid those traps as you approach your ITSM initiatives. The entire book thereafter illustrates with real examples how those principles were applied at different stages of an IT transformation journey.

---

[1]Pink Elephant: http://blogs.pinkelephant.com/index.php?/troy/c/P54/

G. Kahlout, *Spinning Up ServiceNow*, DOI 10.1007/978-1-4842-2571-4_1

Even though the traps are common enough to ITSM and Enterprise Resource Planning (ERP) projects in general, this book is not about general theories; it instead will show how Agile and Lean development methodologies have been applied in ServiceNow by real companies in the real world.

In this chapter:

- Common traps: How a tools mindset and up-front requirements can derail your improvement initiative

- Guiding principles: How humble beginnings and real usage can turn odds in favor of your long-term improvement goals

- Secret weapon: How email can affect successful ServiceNow penetration in the everyday life of your organization

The typical failure story

While it is understandably difficult for management professionals to admit failure and spread the news, numerous studies report a low success rate in ITSM programs in particular, and in enterprise IT programs in general. A report by Service Management consultancy Pink Elephant in 2015 suggested that, in their experience, more than half of ITSM projects failed. Similar remarks have been made by KPMG on ERP projects, where "successful implementation has been notoriously low"[2].

You have probably witnessed this pattern already, where the department ends up abandoning the ITSM tool they invested in, either in favor of another supposedly better tool, or just back to the old way of doing things (usually email). But it's seldom the tool that was the problem, as competing vendors will want you to believe. The true problem of ambitious IT projects is in underestimating the challenge of behavioral change management in achieving sticky users adoption.

ITSM implementors naively expect users' adoption to be a by-product of the tool implementation, a users' manual or initial training plans. They assume that they can force people to abandon email and do it all in the tool.

This may hold true initially, but all too often the initial excitement for the new tool and consultant-drawn ITIL diagrams eventually dies out, usually hand in hand with changes in the management office or in "strategic objectives."

---

[2]https://home.kpmg.com/xx/en/home/insights/2016/02/preparing-for-a-successful-implementation.html

Before we dive into the problem, service management consultant Lee Marshall offers a vivid account of how ITSM projects start and fail, through a fictitious but so typical story. He draws an analogy with Shakespeare's Hamlet and identifies five key acts in the ITSM tragedy. See if you identify with any of them.

Act I: New CIO

Our hero, the Chief Information Officer (CIO), joins an IT organization and, seeing that there is a lack of standardized processes and mistrust between IT and the business, issues the directive that ITIL will be introduced into the organization.

The ITSM program had been successful at the CIO's previous organization, where she had been an IT director, so why couldn't it be successful here?

The directive is for all IT staff to receive ITIL Foundations training and ITSM consultants will be hired to implement ITIL processes.

Act II: Invasion of ITSM consultants

ITIL training is provided in-house to all IT staff. Like most involuntary training involving change, twenty percent of staff will embrace it and get excited about the opportunities ITIL provides, ten percent will be openly hostile to change, and the majority, seventy percent, will take a wait and see attitude. Certificates and pins are handed out, and cute Nerf toys are left behind for people to throw at each other.

Next, ITSM consultants descend on the organization to hold process design workshops, create Visio diagrams and RACI[3] charts and produce ITIL process binders.

An expensive ITSM software tool is chosen and installed with the help of specialists, who can't interpret into the tool the processes designed by the other ITSM consultants, so they configure the tool the way they want to!

The ITSM consultants then leave behind their process designs and documentation, and the organization is left to begin following these processes and using the tool.

Even thought user manuals and training sessions have been offered, management didn't realize what a challenge it was to introduce such a big cultural and operational change.

---

[3]RACI is an accronym for Responsible, Accountable, Consulted, and Informed

Only about 20 percent of people begin following the processes and 20 percent are openly hostile. The rest are indifferent and just wait for this latest management fad to go away so they can go back to working like they always have.

Act III: Incident, Problem, Change,…Stop

The organization starts with implementing the Incident Management process, adds in some service request components, moves on to working on the Problem and a root cause analysis process, and then proceeds to modify their existing Change Management process to align with ITIL. Then…stop.

At this point, the wind begins to die out of the sails of the ITSM program. Champions become disillusioned as they fail to make a business case to move forward with implementing the other ITIL processes. People stop following the processes, if they ever did, since the ITSM consultants never considered how staff would be held accountable for following the processes.

The cultural change associated with ITIL was not considered sufficiently, so no real transformation really happens.

Act 4: Disillusionment

The IT service management program begins to die a slow death. The CIO has other priorities now, primarily outsourcing all IT development to India; the early ITSM champions have left the company, the ITSM software tool is being used for 10 percent of its capability, and duplicate tools are being used and purchased across the organization.

Managed Service Providers (MSPs), also known as IT outsourcers, are approaching the CIO and business unit customers about Software as a Service (SaaS) options for key business processes and Cloud Computing concepts for replacing the organization's costly IT infrastructure.

Act 5: Death

The final act of this tragedy is the death of the ITSM program. The CIO moves on to another organization and the few staff left that believed in the program move on to other projects.

Management and staff who never bought into the program declare it another failed management fad. Ironically, more and more IT systems and functions are outsourced to managed service providers who understand what service management is about. And all that work and effort (and cost) of the ITSM consultants?

The ITIL process binders and documentation sit on shelves and network drives until they are finally discarded as part of a clean-up project.

Common traps

What lessons can be learned from the many failed ITSM projects?

Circumstances will naturally vary from case to case but, just like history repeats itself time and time again (albeit in different places and eras), so do the fundamental factors that cause many ITSM projects to fail.

In fact, in many projects, early signs of failure are typically detected by some people close to the project, but the warnings fail to trigger corrective action.

Many factors are attributed to failed ITSM initiatives, but I herewith will focus on the most fundamental traps I have observed first-hand in my own experience and in the accounts of others.

Clearly identifying those traps with examples, I hope you will then be able to avoid them as you approach your implementation, and resist stakeholders and upper management that propose them. They, of course, will not propose them as "potential traps to sabotage our ITSM project," but they will be framed as opportunities to kill two birds with one stone, or as basic requirements.

1. Tools mindset

Employees who interact with the IT help desk normally do so out of necessity, and when they do, a certain level of tension builds up. Author Nir Eyal tells it bluntly to *Forbes* magazine: "Hating the IT department is a common sentiment in almost every company big enough to have such a group."[4]

There can be many reasons to explain the widespread distaste for IT support, including inadequate staffing, bureaucracy, high turnover, etc... Fundamentally, however, there is also a communication barrier that arises because of the distinctive skill sets and terminology of technical professionals. Failure to appreciate this cultural issue leads some IT managers to put too much stock in the power of new prescriptive policies, processes, and tools supposed to cover up for this underlying issue.

As business author Jim Collins puts it: "The purpose of bureaucracy is to compensate for incompetence and lack of discipline—a problem that largely goes away if you have the right people."[5]

---

[4]Nir Eyal, "Why Everyone Hates IT People": http://www.forbes.com/sites/nireyal/2012/04/13/why-everyone-hates-it-people
[5]Jim Collins, "Good to Great: Why Some Companies Make the Leap...And Others Don't." *HarperBusiness*, 2001, p. 121.

The Information Technology Infrastructure Library (ITIL) service management best practices framework was proposed in 1989, and since then IT departments have been trying to "mature" towards the best-practice ideals theorized in the ITIL books. Hand in hand with ITIL's expansion, vendors of ITIL-based tools have also flourished. In its annual report on the state of the global cloud-based ITSM market, TechNavio research group listed 23 competing vendors of ITSM solutions, including ServiceNow, BMC, and CA in a market estimated to be worth $10–60 billion.[6,7]

Yet, in a 2015 study on the failed outcome of so many ITSM initiatives, service management consultancy Pink Elephant concludes: "failure of many improvement initiatives can be directly attributed to management's lack of understanding that, by implementing processes within traditional hierarchal organizations, they are in reality re-engineering and changing a large part of the IT business culture and accountability structure."[8]

Parallel theories and tools to fundamentally the same problems flourished in the software industry. In order to mitigate the programmer-stakeholder communication issues which jeopardize the successful delivery of software projects within budget and timeline, a slew of best practice recommendations have been proposed, the most notable of which is the Agile development methodology, and best practices such as pair programming and users acceptance testing. Software development life cycle (SDLC) tools also emerged to help teams put those recommendations into practice.

Tools are a welcome part of the solution to IT problems but just like which pencil Stephen King uses to write his bestsellers is not the primary factor in his success as an author, the success of your organization should not be anchored to the tools you use or on the size of your policy documents.

With this understanding, this book does not discuss "how to implement ITIL process X in ServiceNow" but, more fundamentally, how to make of your ServiceNow instance an effective customer service and collaboration platform, that in context encourages desirable people behavior, and ensures consistent and trackable communication with customers.

---

[6]Report on key players in the ITSM software market as of December 2015. Retrieved July 21, 2016. http://www.researchandmarkets.com/research/j7hxbt/global
[7]"What ServiceNow and Salesforce Have in Common." Retrieved January 28, 2016. http://fortune.com/2016/01/28/servicenow-salesforce-annual-revenue-1-billion/
[8]https://www.theitsmhub.com.au/wp-content/uploads/2015/02/Managing-Risks-On-ITSM-Projects.pdf

2. Requirements greed

In typical waterfall implementations of ServiceNow, IT managers are requested to specify up front their requirements for how ServiceNow should be set up for their organization. Development partners will then implement those requirements in ServiceNow, after which the organization will go live with ServiceNow "Phase 1" and start using it.

Because in such a model IT managers have only this opportunity to specify their requirements, they understandably try to squeeze the development agreement by brainstorming every futuristic feature they can imagine to be built in ServiceNow. Otherwise it would feel as if they had left money on the table!

The managers will then say that they embrace a phased approach and have only specified basic processes to launch with ServiceNow in Phase 1, while other requirements will be specified in later phases. In reality, however, Phase 1 requirements are too big a change, anyway, and the phased approach only serves to give them an opportunity to specify later more requirements than they could think of now.

To illustrate, consider these proposed requirements for Al Jazeera's ServiceNow implementation in 2012. At the time, among many all-you-can-eat requirements, the following two requirements were also proposed:

- Interactive Voice Response (IVR) integration, such that when somebody calls the service desk, a ticket is auto-matically logged for the call in ServiceNow
- Automatic tickets assignment based on individual's rota

However, five years on in 2017, neither of those requirements have been implemented, while a completely different set of requirements have.

Another requirement for Phase 1 of the implementation was that users would automatically be logged into ServiceNow if they accessed ServiceNow from a computer connected to the local enterprise network (Single Sign-On). This requirement, which requires a particular integration between ServiceNow and Al Jazeera's login system, was ultimately implemented, but only in 2016.

This does not only occur at Al Jazeeera. A widely-cited study by the Standish Group examined the requirements of thousands of IT projects and then reviewed which of the required features were used in practice.[9] The study found that many requirements end up never being implemented as originally specified, or are implemented but never used in practice, as shown in figure 1-1.

---

[9]https://net.educause.edu/ir/library/pdf/NCP08083B.pdf

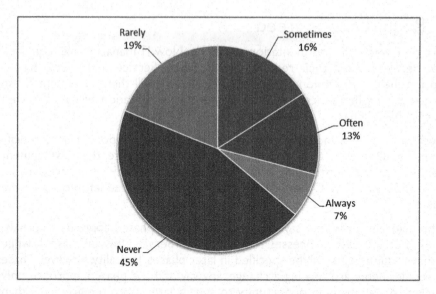

Figure 1-1. The Standish Group study found that almost half of all requirements implemented actually ended up never being used

If those numbers seem excessive to you, you are not alone[10,11] but you may still relate to the co-founder of BaseCamp, Jason Fried's, personal description of the problem:

> "I found project-based consulting frustrating because we would work on a site for months and hand it over to the client, who would inevitably make changes and drag us through their politics. It was rare that what we actually built saw the light of day."

Steve Jobs also offered his advice on the matter: "You have to pick carefully. I'm actually as proud of the things we haven't done as the things I have done. Innovation is saying 'no' to 1,000 things."[12]

When you tell managers about the risk of wasting too much time on requirements that end up not being used in practice, they will defend the requirements with examples as to why those are really needed and how they are guaranteed to deliver tangible value once implemented. Besides that, they are really straightforward to implement in ServiceNow, or the implementation partners said they can be done within a few days, etc.

---

[10]http://www.cs.vu.nl/~x/the_rise_and_fall_of_the_chaos_report_figures.pdf
[11]http://www.drdobbs.com/architecture-and-design/the-non-existent-software-crisis-debunki/240165910
[12]Steve Jobs: "Get Rid Of The Crappy Stuff." Retrieved on November 14, 2016. http://www.forbes.com/sites/carminegallo/2011/05/16/steve-jobs-get-rid-of-the-crappy-stuff

Furthermore, because the most common excuse cited to explain why something goes wrong with an implementation is "poor or changing requirements," business analysts and managers try to thoroughly specify and sign off the requirements, lest they later be accused of causing the whole project to fail.

You can do better, by insisting on like-for-like requirements and small beginnings.

Like-for-like requirements

Rather than debate for months how to collect requirements the right way, ServiceNow provides an illustrative case study of how Echo Entertainment in Australia collected a different type of requirement: like-for-like requirements, so the entire implementation only took three months. More than an implementation, it was a transfer to ServiceNow. As Eric Lewis from Echo puts it: "We used ServiceNow straight out of the box, with just a few configuration changes to ensure that the tool and our processes were aligned."[13]

Like-for-like requirements capture the essence of how things are currently in practice, and build the new tool (ServiceNow) just like that. This way, you are minimizing the friction for people moving from the old tools (email, HPSM, or another set of systems) to ServiceNow.

Note that I don't recommend that you copy the limitations and issues of the current system and force them into the new system, which doesn't have them. Rather, if your current process is simple, it should not be complicated as part of the transfer to the new tool. The story below explains what could go wrong when you do.

To illustrate the perils of launching ServiceNow together with new business processes, consider the story of my first ServiceNow project at Al Jazeera, which did not end up being used as originally intended, despite the political will of management and a successful technical implementation.

Al Jazeera is a global news organization with small and big bureau offices around the world critical for the gathering of news in those places, especially when there are breaking stories. Those bureaus are managed by designated bureau managers that have a monthly budget to pay for deployments, local journalists, and other office expenses. Their finances, HR, and engineering services are handled by regional headquarters, which expect bureau managers to regularly submit to them invoices and request approvals for new expenses and hires.

---

[13]http://www.servicenow.com/content/dam/servicenow/documents/case-studies/cs-echo-201211.pdf

At headquarters, the International Operations Department responsible for the smooth and efficient operation of bureaus complained that many requests were delayed in the process fulfillment, and that for operational continuity reasons it was often necessary to bypass the official processes and, for example, send money to bureaus urgently. Yet it was difficult for the department to track where official requests where getting stuck, and why. Each party in the chain also blamed one another for not adhering to the official processes, for example by not sending all requested invoices, etc.

In order to better track requests and ensure they came in complete and in the right direction, a Service Catalog was built in ServiceNow with forms that bureau managers would have to fill in to make their requests. Once the details were submitted on the portal, the request would automatically be sent for approval from the designated managers, or forwarded to the appropriate department for fulfillment.

Training sessions were provided to bureau managers, and management demanded that all requests be sent through ServiceNow. They even went as far as mandating that the receiving departments of finance and HR should not process any request that is not received through ServiceNow.

Yet, as told in the typical failure story above, most bureau managers seldom used the portal, and the portal was ultimately abandoned, despite the initial will of management and ServiceNow's supposed superiority to email. Why?

Candid bureau managers explained to me that it was easier and faster for them to get their business done over email and, since they were squeezed for time, they did not want to spend it on ServiceNow forms that they considered primarily useful for visibility to management. They argued that if management so dearly wants improved visibility over requests, it should hire a dedicated person to fill out all the forms on ServiceNow.

For the few bureau managers that used the forms, they faced another obstacle; in designing the forms, I had added mandatory fields that stakeholders in the finance departments requested me to add to their forms, but that in reality, it turns out, were seldom provided (such as the tracking number over which the copies of the original expenses were sent).

Bureau managers trying to submit their budget re-consolidation requests on ServiceNow found themselves stuck on a mandatory field they did not have information for (and none thought of filling it with na, not available).

In the end, a full-time administrator was dedicated to fill out the forms on behalf of bureau managers that were responsible for multiple bureaus at once, and this ServiceNow-focused administrator also helped the management at headquarters review an extract reports about requests submitted on ServiceNow. So, some key requests made it into ServiceNow, but not directly by the people intended to use them, and not as frequently.

A like-for-like implementation of ServiceNow in the Al Jazeera case would have started without forms to fill. It would have identified the network of bureau managers and departments emailing each other to fulfill bureau requests, and sought to mirror that on ServiceNow without adding any additional steps or complexity.

Bureau managers would still be able to trigger the request process by firing out an email from their email client (on a desktop or mobile device), but those email conversations would also be mirrored on ServiceNow, as a ticket.

Once they come around to the concept of a unique ticket number for each request, and started referring to the ticket and all conversation about it on ServiceNow as a central source of truth, then request tickets could be upgraded, with approvals, automatic assignments, and forms, etc., based on the reception and feedback of real users in real situations.

Quick wins

One key decision in your ServiceNow implementation is how many ITIL processes you will implement in ServiceNow. In other words, how many different ticket types will your service desk, IT teams, and customers have to deal with?

The temptation is always to start with all the basic ITIL processes of incident management, problem management, and change management. But going by the like-for-like requirements principle, the key question becomes which processes are you already using effectively?

If you are using those processes already, moving to ServiceNow should, of course, not take you a step back and make you abandon some processes.

But to ease the transition and minimize the impact on live operations, you may consider migrating to ServiceNow one process at a time, keeping other things unchanged.

This will shorten the implementation time, and will also make sure that each process in ServiceNow actually delivers value on its own. Note the sharp contrast here with management that claims the benefits of the ServiceNow implementation can be realized only after multiple ITIL processes are implemented together.

Matthias Dieter Hehn from the Volkswagen Group told me that they have implemented in ServiceNow only the Request fulfillment process (further discussed in Chapter 5) and kept Incident management and other ITIL processes in their former tool. The purpose was not to implement ServiceNow per se, it was to deliver business value and, in the case of Volkswagen, the current setup is seen as the best from a cost-benefit analysis perspective.

If, however, your organization does not already keep track of problems separately from incidents, launching ServiceNow with Problem management, even just as it is out of the box, may not work, because the process won't just implement itself in the minds and practices of your people.

Different types of tickets can confuse your support staff, as to which type of ticket to use in which case, and cause duplication. Duplicate tickets—for example, an incident ticket and problem ticket about the same thing—can fragment information and communication lines between the two tickets or lead to lost updates.

At Al Jazeera, when we introduced ServiceNow to the support staff in 2013, it was also accompanied with an out-of-box implementation of Problem management as well. But problem tickets were later abandoned completely, and we hid access to them until 2016 when the department felt better prepared to handle Problem management properly.

From the University of California Davis, IT service manager Ken Jones shared a similar experience. There they launched ServiceNow with Request Fulfillment together with Knowledge and Incident management all at once. But, within weeks, confusion and complaints kicked in and they had to disable Service requests in ServiceNow, abandoned Knowledge, and focused on just using plain simple incident tickets both to record incidents and requests (as Al Jazeera also did). Eventually, both Al Jazeera and UC Davis[14] have implemented the Request fulfillment processes, but one step at a time.

Circumstances may be different in your organization, but I would generally advise you to start using ServiceNow as soon as possible, and with only one process, and iteratively implement new processes and phase out earlier systems driven by business value. In the case of Echo Entertainment, they had a strong incentive to abandon the earlier tool immediately (i.e. an expiring licensing agreement).

3. Management power illusion

When asked, middle management typically shreds off responsibility for the initiative failure on either insufficient executive support or lack of ITIL training at the bottom. But consider again the typical failure story above; if the initiative was endorsed and in fact mandated from the highest management levels, why did it fail nonetheless? Why doesn't management enforce the adoption of the tool and associated processes; couldn't they threaten employees to fill out forms in ServiceNow?

---

[14]http://www.ucop.edu/information-technology-services/award-winners-and-applications/sautter-2014/sautter-ucd-service-oriented-culture.docx

The reality of political power inside organizations is more complex than that.

Some business executives like Jeff Bezos, Donald Trump, and Steve Jobs have built a reputation for placing high and seemingly impossible expectations on their workforce and deploying methods such as intimidation and summary dismissal for those who don't obey.

But, more commonly, management in most organizations have much less leverage on their workforce and cannot force them to do things without risking disrupting smooth business operation, especially in the case of unanticipated events, or risking their positions from escalations about mismanagement. As management consultant Kathy puts it:

"Management of an organization cannot force implementation of a new process or technology. Likewise, management cannot force people to change. Management can create an environment where people simulate change for a period of time. Usually, within a few weeks or months, they revert back to their old way of doing things."

Even Jeff Bezos in the end may succumb to what his workforce presents as the reality of operations, sometimes wasting millions of dollars in the process.

At one point, Bezos got excited about integrating a search engine on Amazon's website that would list products from other online retailers that were not available on Amazon, in return for a commission. So he purchased Junglee, a startup that made this search engine and ordered it be integrated on Amazon's website as "Shop the Web."

But as Brad Stone reports in his book[15] about Bezos, Amazon executives hated the fact that now customers would leave Amazon.com to buy from other retailers, and so the feature ultimately lasted only a few months on the website. As for the reason for this slow death, CEO of Junglee Ram Shiram cites "total tissue rejection," that is, the team didn't buy into it.

The moral of these stories is that top-down support for an initiative is not sufficient. It has worked much less often than people imagine, as rulers and management know. That is why they normally refrain from spending what famed CEO Jack Welsh calls "political capital" on new initiatives. It is better for you not to rely on it.

---

[15]*The Everything Store: Jeff Bezos and the Age of Amazon* (Little, Brown and Company, 2013)

4. ITIL foundation

Training is no doubt important and useful. When a group of people share a common set of beliefs and knowledge, they will be much more motivated to row in the same direction than if the conclusions of that knowledge are imposed upon them.

Some ITIL enthusiasts in the IT department may imagine the ITSM initiative as an opportunity to lecture their customers and colleagues in other departments about ITIL, why they should open an incident, what is the difference between an incident, request or problem, and how they should be given an ultimatum to reply once a ticket is "closed." But that is not the point of Service Management!

ITIL was never meant to be taught to your customers, and ServiceNow should not be seen as a virtual wall between IT staff and the customers you are paid to support.

When ITIL is approached this way, when people reach for support they are now told "please open a ticket," and when they do, their ticket is rejected, and they are told that "this is not an incident, it is a request," and that it should be resubmitted through the portal.

Once they go to this portal to submit their request, they are faced by a maze of options and knowledge articles.

Previously accustomed to quicker support than this, dissent may bubble up to management. Management may also be dismayed by the new IT system because when they requested changes from IT, they have now been told to wait for the Change Advisory Board (CAB) to convene next week and assess the request.

Irritated by such new impairments in supporting the business, I have been told of senior management that turned against the ITSM initiative and mandated that things be simplified back.

It is easy to sympathize with them; they are paying the IT department a certain budget to support the business, not to impair it with apparently bureaucratic processes.

The value of ITIL processes comes from making life recognizably easier for the people you support, treating them like valued customers unconcerned with which agent is on shift, or which team will be involved in fulfilling their request. Tickets should let your support staff easily recall the customer's issue without her having to re-explain it or know the service desk agent she reported it to, or the date and subject of the email she sent.

As Apple puts it introducing the Apple iPad 3: "We believe technology is at its very best when it's invisible. When you're conscious only of what you're doing, not the device you're doing it with."

The same can be said about your ITSM software; at its very best, your customers should not be aware of the underlying ticketing system that you are using to keep track of their support requests.

In an experience-sharing session, CERN Service Manager Reinoud Martens explained how using ServiceNow in non-IT departments showed IT at CERN how those departments sought to "hide the fact that there is an automated process and tickets behind requests and incidents as much as possible," making the system seem "'more human' with special notifications, or service dependent 'signatures.'"[16]

Customer satisfaction definition

Chances are that your department's objectives are stated in terms of maximizing customer satisfaction while also maximizing operational efficiency.

This is exactly what the rest of the business expects from the department. As Jeff Rumburg from MetricsNet reports: *"[customers] want a resolution to their problem or an answer to their question, right then and there! Research across many different industries bears this out. Customer satisfaction—for virtually any type of customer service—strongly correlates with first contact resolution"*[17] (see Figure 1-2).

---

[16]http://www.theitsmreview.com/2013/10/cern/
[17]http://www.thinkhdi.com/~/media/HDICorp/Files/Library-Archive/Insider%20Articles/First%20Contact%20Resolution.pdf

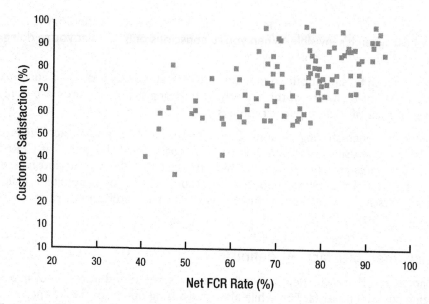

Figure 1-2. There is a strong correlation between resolving the issue of customers right away upon first contact, and their reported satisfaction with customer service

To further illustrate this with a real example from the customer service industry, note how more and more service providers provide help desk support directly on Twitter. Research indeed suggests that: "When an airline responded to a customer's Tweet in less than six minutes, the customer was willing to pay almost 17 more per month for a phone plan if they receive a reply within four minutes."

As shown in Figure 1-3, Turkish Airlines, for example, even makes a public display of how quickly they respond to inquiries sent to them on Twitter[18].

[18]https://blog.twitter.com/2016/study-twitter-customer-care-increaseswillingness-to-pay-across-industries

TWEETS IN LAST 3 HOURS
REPLIED WITHIN
*Shows average reply time. Updated every 5 minutes.
9 Minutes

TWEETS	FOLLOWING	FOLLOWERS	LIKES
126K	52	25.3K	970

Figure 1-3. Twitter page of Turkish Airlines support helpdesk on Twitter, @TK_HelpDesk

Also, Amazon (@AmazonHelp), Dell (@DellCares), and Ford (@FordService) have all been providing support on Twitter for years.

Do not let the ITIL industry shield you from those emerging trends in customer-friendly support.

5. Practical friction

With sufficient motivation, goodwill, and training (or indoctrination) people in your organization may in principle espouse the ITSM initiative and champion use of the proposed tool. Even they however may end up abandoning the tool for practical reasons.

One of the key problems in ITSM and ERP implementations is that when they are introduced in an organization they are introduced together with new and often more rigorous business processes or mandatory fields to fill in forms. While those processes may seem ideal in theory, or suitable at design time, in practice they may not be operable.

Implementers reason that since introducing the new enterprise application will involve development effort and training anyway, they can use the tool implementation project as an opportunity to develop and introduce new business processes as well - a sort of two in one. While this may be desirable, the risks of the project failing are now compounded, since resistance to the new processes and to the new application will be intertwined.

You should be very wary of stakeholders who try to use ServiceNow as a Trojan horse for a new or different process that could not otherwise be put in practice. If the process is impractical or not flexible enough ServiceNow will be abandoned for no fault in the implementation but because the new processes it comes with are incompatible with business reality.

For example, if no formal approval was being collected to get a low-value purchase through but now in ServiceNow a management approval needs to be collected before the process could move forward, uncommunicated issues such as the late availability of the designated approver could prevent the new process from being followed in practice and, consequently, affect ServiceNow, which tied itself to the new approval process. At the very least, every resentment against the new process will be channeled as resentment of ServiceNow, which intertwined itself with the new process. You want to avoid this.

The same could be said of seemingly trivial issues such as the need to authenticate with a password before triggering or approving a process that was previously triggered with a simple managerial email.

Staff may circumvent the system simply because of login issues and the urge to get things done.

It's much safer to phase out change decoupling the tool implementation from the introduction of new more rigorous processes, until people get practically accustomed to ServiceNow in real life operations first.

Email integration

You may think that user engagement is a challenge only for enterprise applications such as ServiceNow because of the work-related nature of the application. But actually user adoption is a key challenge even for social media sites and they deploy various strategies to draw in new members to their network and then keep them coming back. Interestingly, it turns out that social media adoption is driven by email.

In 2010, Facebook acquired a Malaysian startup called Octazen, known for importing contacts from many email providers. Why would Facebook be investing in a company that imports contacts from less popular email providers?

Former growth-team leader at Facebook Chamath Palihapitiya explains that at Facebook they calculated that for a new Facebook user to become engaged she had to befriend at least seven people on Facebook within ten days of creating the account[19]. So access to your email contacts is a valuable way to acquire new members, through the invitation Facebook sends on your behalf.

---

[19]https://blog.modeanalytics.com/facebook-aha-moment-simpler-than-you-think/

Facebook will also send email notifications to your inbox when a friend of yours tags you in a photo or something else happens that may draw you back to Facebook. Until you become a habitually engaged user that checks Facebook on her own.

Other social media sites employ similar strategies, all trying to pull you from your email inbox to their application. Twitter, in addition to personal notifications about people reacting to your tweets also emails you about topics and celebrities that are trending on Twitter.

As of 2012, MediaPost estimates that most social interactions between people online were still done via email and according to Tynt.com, a web sharing plug-in, 80% of links are exchanged via email.[20]

Today's number may be lower but, as an indication of email's continued popularity even outside the corporate world, note how the *New York Times* has a dedicated page that shows which articles have been most shared via email (Figure 1-4).

WORLD	U.S.	N.Y. / REGION	BUSINESS	TECHNOLOGY	SCIENCE	HEALTH	SPO:

| MOST **E-MAILED** | MOST **BLOGGED** » | |

Most E-Mailed Updated Every Fifteen Minutes

Articles most frequently e-mailed by NYTimes.com readers.

| LAST 24 HOURS | LAST 7 DAYS | LAST 30 DAYS |

Figure 1-4. The New York Times website lists which articles have been shared via email the most

If email is so important even for social media engagement, imagine how entrenched email is in corporate culture.

Despite the plethora of enterprise collaboration tools out there, in most organizations email remains the primary medium of written communication and the one through which most organizations' work gets done. For this reason, the most successful project management and enterprise collaboration tools learned to integrate with email and ServiceNow is no exception to this.

---

[20]http://www.mediapost.com/publications/article/181944/quick-whats-the-largest-digital-social-media-pla.html

Basecamp, for example, a popular web-based project management tool not only sends you email notifications about Basecamp activity relevant to you, but it also allows you to update projects and even create new tasks directly from email.

In ServiceNow, a seamless email integration will let your customers open and update ServiceNow tickets for your team via email without even realizing it, and by doing so they will unconsciously spur adoption of ServiceNow at your organization.

You will be maintaining familiar support and communication over email, but with ServiceNow behind the scenes orchestrating the communication's flow (as you define in ServiceNow).

It's a pragmatic approach and somewhat tool-agnostic, but one that should enable you to realize the benefits of ServiceNow as a service management workflow engine while leveraging the familiarity and reach of email. Once people are accustomed, you can also encourage them to use ServiceNow's interfaces, if they wish (as discussed in chapter ten).

Ease of access

If you spend a day with the IT help desk in most organizations you will be struck at how many of the phone calls that they receive are about password resets.

Logins with passwords are also known to hamper purchases and usage of online applications and for this reason many online websites now allow you to log into their service using your Facebook or Microsoft login instead of creating another one with them. Google is also planning to introduce an alternative for passwords in its Android applications to eliminate the user frustration associated with remembering and forgetting passwords.[21]

Also you should avoid having separate passwords for accounts in ServiceNow; and If you synchronize your ServiceNow credentials with your directory server, your ServiceNow users can log in directly with their Windows username and password instead of having to manage and remember different passwords.

A robust LDAP integration between your ServiceNow instance and your directory server can also minimize your day-to-day administrative burden (see chapter 3 for details).

Those were some of the fundamental traps that sabotage IT initiatives approached with inappropriate expectations.

---

[21]https://www.theguardian.com/technology/2016/may/24/google-passwords-android

The next chapter tells of successful ServiceNow implementations, illustrating how you can structure your ServiceNow implementation plan to avoid the common pitfalls described in this chapter.

Tweet-ready take aways

- People, not technology, make an organization successful.

- Resist the temptation to impress your LinkedIn connections with the list of sophisticated ITIL processes that you have introduced.

- Project-based contracts create a situation where you are encouraged to specify requirements that you will not use.

- Changing people's behavior is the real challenge of Service Management, not introducing the latest ITSM tool on the market.

- Rather than debate for months how to collect requirements, collect a different type of requirement: like-for-like requirements.

- ITIL was never meant to be taught to customers, and it should not become a virtual wall between IT staff and those they are paid to support.

- If email is so important even for social media engagement, imagine how entrenched email is in corporate culture.

- A seamless email integration in ServiceNow lets your customers open and update tickets for your team via email without even realizing it.

- People may circumvent the system simply because of login issues, and the urge to get things done.

Innovators' ITSM strategy

How to trace a path of least resistance for ServiceNow at your organization

Chapter 1 described common traps to watch out for when approaching your ITSM initiative and offered pragmatic principles for avoiding them. In this chapter we go further, and review a five-step general implementation strategy that applies the recommended principles.

Understandably, circumstances will vary from organization to organization, and so you may introduce ServiceNow at your organization following a completely different plan. Nonetheless, the proposed plan discussed in this chapter captures the essence of several successful ServiceNow implementations and bears direct relation to a well-researched strategy recognizable in the story of many successful business initiatives in general. As was observed in the research of Harvard business school professor Clayton Christensen, best known as the author of the classic *Innovator's Dilemma*.

Assessing your plan against the implementation strategy proposed in this chapter shall help you recognize potential risks in your plan, and identify paths of least resistance for your implementation plan to proceed more smoothly. After all, one does learn from experience.

© Gabriele Kahlout 2017
G. Kahlout, *Spinning Up ServiceNow*, DOI 10.1007/978-1-4842-2571-4_2

Take legendary Benjamin Franklin for example. In his classic auto-biography,[1] he describes how he observed from experience the "impropriety of presenting one's self as the proposer of any useful project that might be supposed to raise one's reputation in the smallest degree above that of one's neighbors, when one has need of their assistance to accomplish that project."

Benjamin then found a way to propose his useful projects without stirring much envy from his peers and temporarily sacrificing his vanity. He then recalls how "in this way my affair went on more smoothly, and I ever after practiced it on such occasions, and, from my frequent successes, can heartily recommend it." The same goes for the general strategy proposed in this chapter; it is tried-and-tested and, as we shall see with examples from Al Jazeera and other customers, I can heartily recommend it.

In this chapter:

- Where to start: How to pick the first users to start your ServiceNow revolution and make your quick win. It probably should not be your main IT help desk.

- When and how to expand: How to know if it is time to expand ServiceNow to other teams, and how to do it under favorable conditions that will let you win in the expectations game.

Overview

In his research, Professor Christensen pondered how come so many great companies fail epically so many times, while new competitors apparently emerging out of the blue consistently manage to out-compete the established incumbents despite fewer resources and un-established reputation. Management was certainly not "stupid,"[2] but Christensen observed flaws in the decision-making process of established market leaders that actively discard the initially modest ideas that smaller competitors instead nurture to great success.

He observed that disruptors like Netflix's movies-by-mail business for example do not start by competing head-on with incumbent market leaders in Blockbuster-like movie rental shops. Netflix instead first went after an underserved niche: People looking for unpopular films and willing to wait for their delivery over the mail.

---

[1]Benjamin Franklin, *Autobiography of Benjamin Franklin*, 1793
[2]http://harvardmagazine.com/2014/07/disruptive-genius

The same pattern could be observed in Toyota's inexpensive Corolla cars, Sony's Walkman portable stereo, and Uber's good-enough alternative to car ownership for some people.

Examining real-world case studies such as these Christensen identified that they all followed a similar pattern, dubbed the innovator's solution. In a nutshell, and in my own words the tried-and-tested solution observed was to:

1. Start with easy-to-please customers at the outskirts of the market;

2. Observe what jobs customers hire the product for and improve it for those specific circumstances;

3. Patiently but profitably capture opportunities to climb upmarket, satisfying more customers from the bottom up;

4. Emerge as an irresistible mainstream offering, while it is too late for established competitors to battle you.

In the first two steps management pursues an emerging strategy, not yet committing to a plan for market dominance.

Only after going live with profitable small customers and setting up a cost structure that is pleased with those low-hanging fruit opportunities a proven strategy emerges to dominate the market.

Emphasizing the importance of pursuing this iterative strategy Christensen notes: "Research suggests that in over 90 percent of all successful new businesses, historically, the strategy that the founders had deliberately decided to pursue was not the strategy that ultimately led to the business's success."[3] Their ability to identify what works and switch gears is what enabled them to succeed nonetheless.

Intel Corporation for example, started as a manufacturer of memory chips (DRAM) and it took a while for management at Intel to realize that microprocessors instead (at first made for a calculator project) were going to be the future of the business.

The five-step strategy outlined above is, of course, not the only way to win in a market; One could skip all the way to step three and offer mainstream customers arguably superior products. But Christensen's analysis found that this is precisely what large organizations have almost always done before they failed.

---

[3]Christensen, Clayton M., *The Innovator's Solution: Creating and Sustaining Growth*, Harvard Business Review Press, 2013

Put simply, you have thin chances of success competing for mainstream customers from the start and a high risk of losing your upfront investments, while those that start from the outskirts with modest plans tend to have more success in the end. Management can have huge visions in both cases, the difference is in the approach only.

In my own research I found remarkable similarity between Christensen's analysis of failed product launches and failed ITSM initiatives: Smart and competent people on both sides, the same unexpected yet common failed outcome. Furthermore, I could identify Christenen's solution pattern in the things that worked in our ServiceNow implementation at Al Jazeera and verified the same with other ServiceNow customers and case studies.

Based on this insight, I propose a ServiceNow implementation strategy that could be used as the basis for your patient-but-revolutionary ServiceNow implementation, if you manage to convince management of it and resist big-bang temptations.

Step 1: Pick your customers

The internal customers to whom you first offer ServiceNow matter a lot as they may become active advocates or doom the initiative. By internal customer I mean teams that will use ServiceNow to handle their daily operations work.

As Christensen notes, successful innovators avoid the obvious customer for their product as those will be invested in another system.

Even though ServiceNow may be arguably better the switch can be slow and packed with challenges, and politics. A much better starting point is to find either:

1. Internal customers that are not using a software system yet but have grown in need for one;

2. Internal customers that have abandoned a software system not because it lacks advanced features, but because they needed something simpler and easier to use. (Note how this is different than offering them something that is more functional than their current system.)

Customers like these will eagerly accept ServiceNow for its core functionality and will have a low baseline to compare it with (email and spreadsheets, or a legacy system they didn't fully use).

The diagram in Figure 2-1 schematically illustrates how to identify your initial ServiceNow users, while the examples below illustrate how this unfolds in the real world.

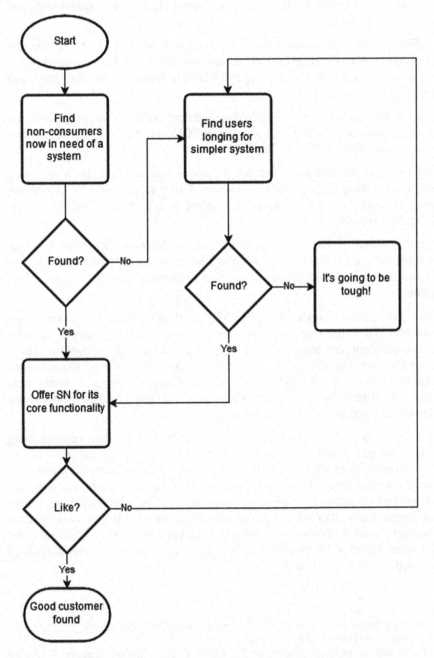

Figure 2-1. It's easier to start from customers that desire ServiceNow for its core functionality. Seek them first

Examples

At Al Jazeera, the central IT help desk was not the first internal customer to use ServiceNow. It was the fourth, almost a year after other departments and teams had been using it.

At CERN, winner of ServiceNow's Innovation Award in 2011,[4] it was the non-IT general services department that has been cited for triggering the ServiceNow project, while replacing the Remedy system in the IT department did not go live until 2013.[5]

As said in the earlier chapter, the Volkwsagen group, which made a presentation of its ServiceNow Services catalog in 2013, has not yet migrated other ITIL processes from HPSM to ServiceNow.

The more case studies you consider, the more you will find this a recurring pattern with many ServiceNow customers. This helps explain ServiceNow's expansion outside the traditional IT market and into so-called Enterprise Service Management.

To further illustrate the challenge faced by introducing ServiceNow head-on as a replacement for an existing ticket system that the IT department is used to, consider how the widespread adoption of ServiceNow at Al Jazeera first unfolded.

At Al Jazeera, even though the central IT help desk openly complained about its current ITSM tool replacing their system came with many pre-conditions often dependent on improvements in other tools (e.g. ActiveDirectory), agreements with other teams and business users, and inflated expectations about what ServiceNow should offer from the get-go (e.g. a smart rota system that automatically assigned tickets based on workload and skill). There was a lot of discussion - and a stalemate.

The IT system and network teams, by contrast, had already started using ServiceNow to log and keep track of major changes they planned to make to the IT infrastructure. What made it easy for them to start using ServiceNow's Change Management tickets right away and without pre-conditions was that they needed to prove that they had planned and obtained approval before making potentially risky infrastructure changes, or ones that involve downtime of business critical services, and they had no system for that. Engineers and team leads found in ServiceNow's change request tickets an official-enough reference to cover their backs.

---

[4]ServiceNow Innovation of the Year Award, retrieved on 20-Nov-16. http://www.servicenow.com/innovation.html#Winner5

[5]R. Alvarez Alonso, et al., "Migration of the CERN IT Data Centre Support System to ServiceNow," *Journal of Physics: Conference Series* 513, 2014

Outside IT, a non-IT department in the business was interested in centralizing their communication channels with international bureaus under one system. As told in Chapter 1, it was not easy to launch ServiceNow there either but within a few months a nine-forms Requests catalog for shared services was eventually rolled out (see Figure 2-2).

Figure 2-2. Promotional graphic of nine-form service catalog launched for a non-IT department as first Requests user of ServiceNow

Then again, another group in the IT department got interested in ServiceNow. Senior management in the IT department was looking for a solution to better manage the department's many contracts and their renewal process ahead of the contracts' end dates.

Acknowledging the need for some system and not having one, management was interested in using ServiceNow as a searchable repository of the department's contracts and to trigger scheduled reminders to specific people to remind them of the contract renewal process. So it was that limited-scope Contracts Management in ServiceNow was rolled up, even before Incident Management was.

Then came a new big customer for ServiceNow, from the United States. Al Jazeera had acquired Current TV to launch its new Al Jazeera America (AJAM) channel and integration works were to be completed before the new channel would go live on air. As part of this integration, AJAM management wanted better visibility of all support requests received and still-pending action. A shared inbox was just not enough for them.

There had been a ticketing system but it was seldom used, while most support requests were sent through by email to a team of super-busy technical heroes who were also working on the channel setup. Offering to integrate ServiceNow with email, ServiceNow was again seen as a better alternative to the status quo.

Step 2: Set expectations

In picking your initial customers, I recommended that you go after customers whose expectations can be met with ServiceNow as it is Out-Of-Box (OOB).

In defining the initial scope for the implementation with them you should also make sure that by using ServiceNow they are not outstretching the level of complexity that they are already used to handle in their previous system.

Even if ServiceNow can do it OOB, offering all ITIL processes to a team that just used email conversation for all their issues, problems, and feature requests can be overwhelming. As Gustav Hoyer, former IT director at Sony Pictures puts it: "ServiceNow is incredibly agile. You don't have to worry about scalability; you just need to make sure the functionality is rolling out at a rate that human beings can absorb."[6]

As such, you can use this criteria to determine what should be in-scope and out of it for the implementation project:

1. How close is the proposed scope to ServiceNow's core functionality (OOB)?

2. How close is it in terms of complexity to what the customer is already familiar with and actively using?

The diagram in Figure 2-3 schematically illustrates how to identify the initial scope for a ServiceNow launch, after which an example is given from Al Jazeera America's implementation of ServiceNow.

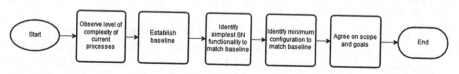

Figure 2-3. Define appropriate scope for initial ServiceNow launch

Initial scope

When ServiceNow was launched to the support teams at Al Jazeera America (AJAM) the purpose was to have a single system of record for support staff to collaborate on and track issues until their successful resolution, and to have an accessible archive for later reference and analysis. So the scope of the implementation was limited to:

---

[6]https://www.servicenow.com/content/dam/servicenow/other-documents/ebook/downloads/Sony_Pictures_Automate_the_IT_Value_Chain.pdf

Users

The newly-formed technology teams in New York and other support hubs across the United States, supporting Al Jazeera's America's staff only.

Processes

Teams were to keep following their established processes, the execution of which was currently being tracked in email conversations and manually populated spreadsheets. ServiceNow was expected to facilitate the execution of those processes.

Baseline

Prior to ServiceNow staff could easily reach staff over email, in person, or over the phone. All support staff had access to a shared mailbox and were able to instantly assist the customer.

Using ServiceNow should not involve more labor on any part (end-user or supporter) in requesting support or providing it. The added traceability and order of tickets in ServiceNow was expected to provide more consistent handling of tickets and fewer instances of neglected aging tickets, and reduce the impact of "who shouts the loudest."

Goals

As you can imagine, launching ServiceNow management also envisioned the ability to launch Change Management in ServiceNow, a request portal, as well as other ITIL processes as part of the launch. Below is only a subset of the goals that were stipulated for the launch, but more usefully, it is those that were actually achieved:

1. Collaboration: Support staff in America effectively manage their individual work queues, as well as distribute work amongst teams more effectively than over emails using an easy-to-use an collaboration system (ServiceNow).

2. Traceability: Supervisors have visibility over all work being handled by the support organization with the ability to peek into particular trouble areas (e.g., ageing tickets).

3. Fit for purpose: ServiceNow basic interfaces are customized to fit what works for AJAM's support workflows and needs.

4. Access control: AJAM support staff accessed ServiceNow using their Al Jazeera credentials and could self-manage access to ServiceNow without need of external expertise.

5. Automation: Emails sent to the support email address were received by ServiceNow and automatically converted into tickets, freeing requesters and support staff from having to open a ticket for support requests received by email.

6. Callers' experience: Asking for support and interacting with support staff should remain straightforward, and requesters should find the email notifications they receive appropriate in content and frequency.

Step 3: Minimal setup

The setup to start managing incidents in ServiceNow at its minimum would only involve configuring users' access to ServiceNow, but would typically also include configuring email notifications, assignment groups, and a few customizations like setting categories and locations.

To guide implementors through the setup there is in ServiceNow an ITSM Guided Setup that takes them through a 12-step setup (see Figure 2-4) to:

- Map your organization's structures in ServiceNow: users, groups, locations, departments, companies, etc.;

- Configure connections with your email and authentication servers;

- Define categories, assignment workflows, date formats, mandatory fields, Service-Level Agreements, etc.;

- Set up a Service Portal, design forms, and management dashboards.

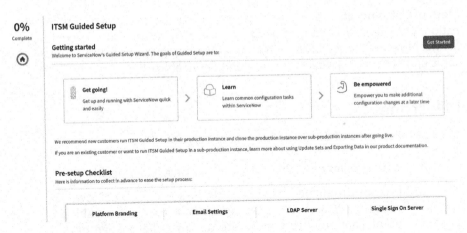

Figure 2-4. ITSM guided setup in ServiceNow

For guidance at an architectural level, Part 2 of the book goes over your options for managing users' access (Chapter 3), routing incoming emails appropriately (Chapter 4), and sending elegant email notifications (Chapter 5). Chapter 6 shows you examples of Service Portals, and Chapter 7 talks about how to make reporting useful for all at all levels.

Step 4: Go live quickly

On its website ServiceNow showcases Pacific Aluminum from Brisbane, Australia for having completed its implementation project within 30 days, but going live within eight days of starting the project.[7]

At Al Jazeera America a few months passed between project start and actual deployment but most of that time was actually spent on other activities, waiting, and supporting existing non-AJAM users on ServiceNow.

Other ServiceNow customers also report taking months in negotiation and preparation for the launch.

As the AJAM channel launch on air approached I was flown to New York to fast-forward the go-live with ServiceNow. Once on-site, it took ten days to go live with a minimal setup.

---

[7]http://www.servicenow.com/content/dam/servicenow/documents/case-studies/cs-pacific-aluminium.pdf

Most of the time on-site was not even spent on the tool, it was on coordination, training, and hand-holding after go-live. AJAM officially started using ServiceNow before the LDAP integration was complete, as it took a while to set it up between Al Jazeera's servers and ServiceNow's.

Milestones

The key milestones of the implementation were:

1. User profiles of AJAM staff are all available in ServiceNow.

2. Each of the support staff in AJAM logs into ServiceNow with their Windows logins, knows how to see all AJAM tickets, and how to collaborate on any ticket (assign or update).

3. Support staff has access and knows how to revoke or grant same access to new members in the team.

4. Email notifications are sent successfully on behalf of the Service Desk to the right people about new and updated tickets.

5. Emails sent to the Support email address are successfully received in ServiceNow to create new tickets automatically, or update existing ones.

6. Ability to monitor instance and correct functioning, ability to immediately restore smooth operations with alternative solution, and tight control over changes that could impact multiple users in ServiceNow.

Numerous other ServiceNow customers who spoke at the ServiceNow knowledge conferences or are showcased by ServiceNow were able to go live within weeks. This is not a feature of their smartness or resources, or even maturity; it is often a reflection of how small their scope was and how few customizations they made.

Back to the Sony Pictures example which launched within 60 days, Gustav Hoyer said: "We are not going to customize the tool. We are going to use ServiceNow as is and assume that has been battle-tested. This is how incident works, end of discussion."

In online journalism, the mantra coined by news media expert Jeff Jarvis is "Publish first, edit later" while in the *Art of the Start 2.0*,[8] the former chief Apple evangelist promotes the concept of *"Don't worry be crappy"* as an invitation to ship products early, even if they are far from perfect, and then based on actual feedback, improve it.

In case you wonder if Apple used to do this too, consider how the first iPhone did not support 3G Internet browsing while other Nokia phones did at the time, for example. The first iPhone was revolutionary in many ways, and backward in a few mainstream features.

Also note how the first iPhone only allowed third-party contribution as Safari Internet browser extensions. But then it changed course, and instead released developer tools and APIs to develop apps, and released the App Store.

The idea from launching early is that when real people use your product in real-world situations, you can observe how they use it and not use it, and make it better for real. This suits ServiceNow very well, given how flexible it is to customize after go-live (see Part 3 for after-go live guidance).

Step 5: Refine and emerge

After going live with ServiceNow at Al Jazeera America, I stayed there to assist the teams using ServiceNow, observe what was not practical or caused confusion, and fine-tuned ServiceNow to fit the job better.

It is important to note that at AJAM there was a daily stream of new people joining and that had to use ServiceNow, so we could not rely on expecting them to remember how to do the right thing. We had to make doing the right thing the default thing to do.

Throughout the book and in Chapter 11 you will find details of changes made to ServiceNow in the pursuit of eliminating room for error and encouraging the desired behavior, as ServiceNow usage grew globally.

How do you know if people are actually using ServiceNow effectively? Reports in ServiceNow (Chapter 7) can measure different aspects of ServiceNow usage to determine what is not being used effectively, or who it is who is not using it. From there you can decide to simplify procedures, change defaults, or approach the people in question.

---

[8]Guy Kawasaki, *The Art of the Start 2.0: The Time-Tested, Battle-Hardened Guide for Anyone*, Penguin books, 2015

After the successful launch of ServiceNow at AJAM, there was more appetite for using ServiceNow by the core teams in Doha, and many of the earlier hurdles disappeared. Something like ServiceNow at AJAM was now considered sufficient, and in fact desirable.

The more teams signed up to use ServiceNow, the more people interacting with those teams received neat email notifications sent from ServiceNow about their ticket's status (see Chapter 5). The word spread quickly and more teams and managers asked to use ServiceNow in their team.

Then HR teams also got interested in using it to track their requests and collaborate on issues with ERP teams.

In the end, ServiceNow had emerged as a mainstream corporate application used daily, while the discourse changed from "What are all the things ServiceNow should be able to do before it can be beneficial to us" to "Why are not we on ServiceNow also?!"

This is what I also hope for your implementation. It takes patience and comes with uncertainty as to how exactly things will unfold, but if it works it will be worth it.

As you on-board more teams, new issues show up that can jeopardize current users or hinder new ones (e.g., confidentiality). Part 3 of this book proposes solutions to common issues faced at this stage.

Tweet-ready takeaways

- It's easier to start with customers who desire ServiceNow for its core functionality. Seek them first.

- Those starting modestly from the outskirt tend to succeed in the end. They too can have huge visions, the difference is in the approach only.

- Change the discourse from "What are all the things ServiceNow should do before it can be beneficial to us" to "Why are not we on it also?!"

- Big things have small beginnings. Going live quickly is not a feature of maturity, it is a reflection of how small the scope is.

- When real people use your product in real-world situations, you can observe how they use it and not use it and make it better for real.

- Push out quickly, follow up, make corrections, push again, make corrections, push again, and so forth.

Essentials

Action is the foundational key to all success.

—Pablo Picasso

Part I made a case for going live with the minimum configuration possible. Here is what needs setup, whatever teams or processes you go live with.

Rather than a chore setup, Part II casts the light on opportunities to reduce friction for users on both ends of a ServiceNow ticket.

Although more technical than Part I, in Part II we cover basics that being aware of as the manager in charge of ServiceNow will help you safeguard it from breaches and ensure spam is not sent on your behalf.

ServiceNow comes with a Guided ITSM Setup module to guide your administrator in the setup. This part of the book is a similar guide, but at a functional level to give you an understanding of key aspects of ServiceNow and insight to effectively oversee it after go-live, as well.

Chapter 3: User accesss

Chapter 4: Email support

Chapter 5: Elegant notifications

Chapter 6: Request portal

Chapter 7: Reporting

User access

What you need to know about access in ServiceNow

This chapter is the first of five chapters intended to help you as the project manager of a ServiceNow implementation prepare for the go-live.

In this chapter you will get an overview of how users profiles will be created and updated in ServiceNow, and considerations that will affect user administration after go-live.

In this chapter:

1. Types of users: What presence in ServiceNow is needed for your end-users;

2. Efficient users administration: How to efficiently grant (and revoke) access to new members and teams getting on ServiceNow;

3. Access levels: Who has access to what, and how to protect users data;

4. Stability Considerations: What if things break;

5. ServiceNow licenses: How access roles affect your ServiceNow contractual implications;

© Gabriele Kahlout 2017
G. Kahlout, *Spinning Up ServiceNow*, DOI 10.1007/978-1-4842-2571-4_3

In ServiceNow's Guided ITSM Setup, one of the first steps is LDAP integration (Figure 3-1). LDAP is an IT acronym for Lightweight Directory Access Protocol which basically lets an application like ServiceNow access users profiles in your organization's directory server, usually Active Directory by Microsoft.

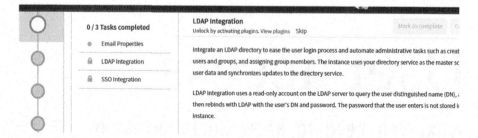

Figure 3-1. LDAP integration is a step in ServiceNow's basic ITSM Guided setup.

For your Servicedesk to effectively log and manage tickets in ServiceNow everyone in your organization will need to have a user profile in ServiceNow even if they will never log in.

This is because in order to log a ticket for someone in your organization and provide them with updates about her ticket over email, there first needs to be a selectable user profile for her in ServiceNow (see Figure 3-2).

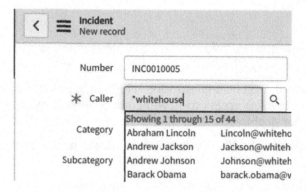

Figure 3-2. Every incident in ServiceNow needs to be logged against a user profile already in ServiceNow.

With the LDAP integration, you automatically sign up everyone into ServiceNow and reduce the overhead of user administration in ServiceNow by a large degree.

Without an LDAP integration, it is still possible to create user profiles automatically every time someone from your organization emails support and a ticket is opened automatically (see next chapter for tickets via email). So if after reading this chapter you decide that LDAP integration is not feasible for your circumstances, you still have an option to create user profiles on the fly (see Figure 3-3).

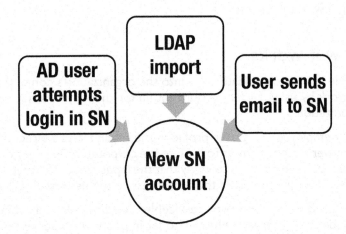

Figure 3-3. Cases in which a new user account with limited access is automatically created in ServiceNow.

With the LDAP integration setup however it will be much simpler to log tickets for anyone, and richer user profiles will be imported in ServiceNow with details such as the full name, phone number, title, and location (if those details are recorded in your LDAP server).

LDAP integration automatically updates ServiceNow every time user profiles are updated in your directory server. From a maintenance prospective, this is a big plus.

Savvy end users will also be able to log into ServiceNow and preview all of their support requests, while all users will have tickets logged against their accounts without them needing to know what ServiceNow is and that they have an account in it.

LDAP integration

ServiceNow comes with built-in support for the integration with Active Directory servers and ServiceNow's official documentation provides a comprehensive walk-through of all the steps involved in a standard integration.

Nonetheless, the integration is still a fairly complex setup and requires collaboration between your Active Directory administrators, network team and your ServiceNow administrator.

Appendix C lists detailed technical requirements and prerequisites to import and sync user profiles from your organization's directory servers, and to provide your support team members with adequate access. Here is a high-level overview of the process.

How it works

People in your organization log into the organization's computers or wireless network by using a user account set up for them by IT when they joined the organization.

Every employee has a user profile in the organization's directory servers and whenever a user attempts to log into the corporate Wi-Fi their device connects to those directory users to verify that the input credentials match those stored in the directory servers. If they do, access to the network is granted.

The LDAP integration with ServiceNow enables ServiceNow to check with your directory servers whether to let in people into ServiceNow or not. So when an employee attempts to log into ServiceNow, ServiceNow connects to your directory servers and verifies if the input credentials are correct. If so, the user is granted access to ServiceNow.

ServiceNow could also import from your directory servers the user profiles of your employees including details such as email address, location, department, and full names. It could also import group membership details, to know to which user groups the employee belongs.

So besides authentication at the time of login ServiceNow also regularly connects to your directory servers and imports new user profiles into ServiceNow and updates existing ones.

A good thing about the LDAP integration in ServiceNow is that it is only one way, from your directory servers to ServiceNow. That is, ServiceNow will only read user profiles from your LDAP servers but will never create or overwrite data in there. This guarantees the integrity of users' data in directory servers.

Unique ID

When setting up the integration you will need to decide how to uniquely identify users. That is based on which unique field ServiceNow should use to create a new user profile, or update an existing one.

By default, ServiceNow will identify users by their username (samaccount-name in Active Directory), but if your LDAP servers host users from multiple domains (e.g., @aljazeera.com and @subsidiary.org) or if your organization later changes the format of usernames, for example from firstname.lastname to lastname+ initials, or if you change your primary email domain, then the mechanism will fail.

In such scenarios users may be duplicated in ServiceNow while tickets will remain associated with the account with the old email address.

If this applies to you, you should be careful not to use the email address or username to identify and match user profiles; Instead match profiles based on a unique and immutable field ID in your LDAP server (e.g., the objectSID).

End users don't need to know about this, it's just something to be set up behind the scenes for the integration to work smoothly.

Security

ServiceNow describes the read-only LDAP integration as secure because it connects "from a single machine that uses a fixed IP address through a specific port on the firewall."[1]

But if you would rather use LDAPS (secure LDAP), you can also do that by uploading a public certificate to be used by ServiceNow for encrypting messages to your directory server.

Alternatively, you can set up a VPN between ServiceNow and your network so that traffic between the two ends is secured by the VPN. At Al Jazeera we use VPN.

As soon as an account is disabled in Active Directory that user will no longer be able to log into ServiceNow. This is because every login attempt in ServiceNow is verified against Active Directory and if the AD servers reply to ServiceNow that the user is disabled the login will not go through.

The disabled user will continue to be sent emails from ServiceNow but they will probably not be received because the mailbox will be disabled or inaccessible.

---

[1]https://docs.servicenow.com/bundle/helsinki-servicenow-platform/page/integrate/ldap/reference/r_SecureLDAPConnections.html

Temporary accounts

When accounts are created at your organization for freelancers or interns, they may be created with an expiration date after which the account gets automatically disabled.

ServiceNow by default does not check for this expiration date field and thus the account will indefinitely remain active in ServiceNow until manually disabled, perhaps also affecting your ServiceNow subscriptions totals (discussed below). You can however customize ServiceNow to automatically disable accounts based on the expiration date.

Performance

Performance can be an issue for large organizations with thousands of users.

To mitigate the performance impact of scheduled synchronizations between directory servers and ServiceNow, ServiceNow recommends that you schedule the sync once daily and outside peak hours.

Syncing only once a day means that updates to user details will not take effect until the sync occurs the next day, unless the individual user profile is individually refreshed from ServiceNow on an on-demand basis.

ServiceNow technical online documentation also lists other optimizations recommendations (such as paging) to speed up the synch.

Availability

In the event that your directory server is down, what do you do?

It won't be possible for your users to log into ServiceNow but it probably would also be a bigger problem for the entire organization because they will be unable to access other critical systems that also rely on the directory, like email.

In any case, ServiceNow lets you specify a redundant LDAP server to check with in case the primary LDAP server is inaccessible and your organization has more than one LDAP server.

In the event that ServiceNow fails to connect with your directory servers, ServiceNow can also send an email notification to the users you specify in a group called LDAP Admins group (see Figure 3-4).

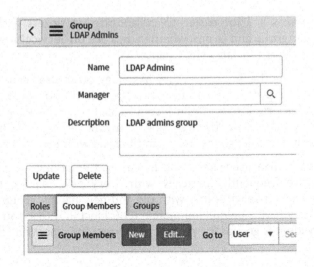

Figure 3-4. Out-of-box users group to be notified in case of LDAP connection issues.

You also want to make sure that there is a ServiceNow local administrator account that is not an LDAP user so that you may at least log into ServiceNow using that account to resolve the LDAP issues (e.g., update LDAP configuration settings in ServiceNow).

Groups sync

In addition to synchronizing user accounts you could also synchronize user groups.

Every team at your company will most likely have a user group in Active Directory and when new people join the organization they are added to the groups with which they need to collaborate with. Instead of recreating and maintaining those groups in ServiceNow you could have groups in ServiceNow synchronize with those in Active Directory.

There are many benefits for automatically importing groups in ServiceNow:

1. It eliminates the friction that results from having to recreate groups in ServiceNow and update them manually in ServiceNow.

2. It eliminates the need for managing group memberships in ServiceNow; It will be all done in Active Directory and automatically reflected in ServiceNow.

3. It makes it a lot easier to collaborate on tickets with other group and teams, whether they are on ServiceNow already or not (also see Chapter 10).

However, it may be that your directory has many other user groups that are meant for internal processes and that most people do not know about and do not email. Importing them in ServiceNow can make things a bit messier than ideal and it may be worth discussing with your directory administrators a solution to filter those groups out from the sync with ServiceNow.

Also, even more than usernames, the names and email IDs of groups tend to change more frequently (basically with every new manager). To avoid duplicating groups in ServiceNow with old and new names, group profiles in Active Directory have a unique immutable ID (objectSID) that you can use to unequivocally identify groups for your Active Directory sync with ServiceNow.

Location OUs

How do you determine the location of the user?

Directory servers often provide a field to store the location and address but this is seldom accurate, standardized, or even uniformly populated for all users.

However, in many directory servers users tend to be segregated in so called Organizational Units and those OUs normally represent a location, or department.

For example a user profile may be contained in all of IT, Doha, and AwesomeOrg OUs.

Other users will belong to different OUs but all users located in Doha, Qatar will also belong to the Doha OU. Users in New York Manhattan will be in the NYM OU, and so on. Also no user can belong to two geographic OUs.

So in ServiceNow, you can create locations that match the OUs so that they are updated directly from LDAP.

Single Sign-On

Single Sign-On in ServiceNow is one of the steps listed in the ITSM Guided Setup with built-in support in ServiceNow.

Single Sign-On basically means that people at your organization will need to authenticate only once to use your organization's networks and applications, and that they will do this through one single login screen unified across all applications in your organization.

In other words, users wanting to access ServiceNow will not have to log in because they have already authenticated with your corporate network.

Or if they have not, ServiceNow will redirect them to authenticate with your organization's login screen, instead of ServiceNow's. SSO eliminates the need to log in with corporate applications, and allows for a more seamless user experience.

As with the LDAP integration, configuring ServiceNow with SSO is not a configuration on ServiceNow's end only but requires support from your system and network teams.

At Al Jazeera, we had an implementation of SSO that was incompatible with ServiceNow and it took considerable setup (and more than two years) before we got one that worked with ServiceNow.

Access levels

The basic LDAP integration will enable users to have an account in ServiceNow and be able to log in. But they will not have any privileged access in ServiceNow and cannot manage or assign tickets. Those privileged access assignments need to be configured in ServiceNow.

As of the Istanbul release of ServiceNow, there are over one hundred out-of-box access roles that a ServiceNow administrator could grant (see Figure 3-5).

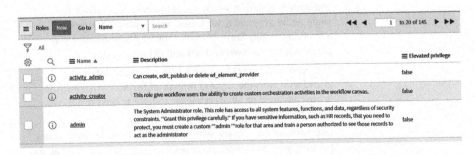

Figure 3-5. There are over 100 user roles in ServiceNow.

Each role grants fine-tuned access to particular areas of the application that you may not need to know about until you need to, but Table 3-1 below describes the key five access roles that you should be aware of.

Managing users, access it is important that you:

1. Regularly verify who has administrator access, as they could delete all records on your instance;

2. Insist that access is not assigned directly to individual users but is instead granted through membership in groups that need the access;

3. Make sure you grant access roles in accordance with your licensing agreement;

Associating access privileges with user groups instead of individuals directly allows you to ensure consistent access roles for all members of the group. It also automatically grants and revokes access based on membership in the team.

For example, the user_admin role can be assigned to your Servicedesk group in ServiceNow so that each member of the Servicedesk automatically gets it so long as they are in the group. This makes access roles much more consistent and manageable and reduces the likelihood for users to have more or less access roles than expected.

Basic access levels

Table 3-1 shows the five key access roles in ServiceNow.

Table 3-1. Five key access roles in ServiceNow

Access Role	Description
No role and snc_internal	A user account with no assigned roles can log into ServiceNow and update tickets in which she is involved. She cannot for example be assigned tickets, view ticket queues assigned to a team, or modify ServiceNow in any way, beyond minimally personalizing her own account and tickets view.
	Your end users may also have a role called snc_internal, introduced with the Geneva release of ServiceNow. This role is now assigned to all users meant to have at least the above-described access to the system.
	Users without a role (or with snc_internal) usually don't count towards your subscriptions count - you can have as many as you want.
approver_user	Users with this role can approve (or reject) items for which their approval has been requested. Otherwise users without this role cannot approve requests!
	If a user has no other role but this role it will be counted as an approver license which is counted separately from the standard fulfiller license.

(continued)

Table 3-1. (continued)

Access Role	Description
itil	This is the basic role granted to those meant to actively use ServiceNow, assigning and managing ticket queues. With the ITIL role they can view and modify any ticket logged in ServiceNow as well as be assigned a ticket. They can also view and run reports but they cannot delete tickets or modify ServiceNow beyond personalizing their own view of tickets or modifying tickets content.
	Users with the ITIL role and any other role that grants similar access to view lists of records normally count as a fulfiller subscription.
user_admin	Confers on its holder the ability to create, modify, or delete users, groups, locations, and company records in ServiceNow.
admin	This is the super user role in ServiceNow. A user with the administrator role can make changes on the application that are immediately visible to everyone.

The ITIL role is the access level intended for people expected to manage tickets in ServiceNow. Anyone with it can view any ticket in ServiceNow.

There is no such thing as confidentiality in ServiceNow out-of-box (see Chapter 9 for alternatives); Anyone with ITIL access can view and participate on any ticket in ServiceNow.

The user_admin role instead may be conferred to your Servicedesk team to manage users and groups in ServiceNow, while the admin role (capable of deleting all records) should be granted very restrictively.

A personal story illustrates how harmful the admin role can be on a production environment:

One day, I accidentally deleted my home page in ServiceNow. Normally when an itil user deletes his home page it only affects his view in ServiceNow and ServiceNow will automatically set for him the default home page for itil users.

But when I did it as an admin, I had accidentally deleted the home page for all itil users! And I got called on the issue within five seconds of it occurring. The Servicedesk group were no longer able to view their tickets queue.

Fortunately I was able to restore the home page within minutes by copying from another non-production instance where the same home page was configured (refer to Chapter 8 for advice on managing your ServiceNow environments), but you get the point!

Using ServiceNow with the admin role is risky and can wreak havoc for all users. An admin user that doesn't need the role in his day-to-day activity may be better off having a separate dedicated admin account to be used on a need basis only.

Managing licenses

How licenses are counted may depend on your particular contract with ServiceNow, so you need to verify the information provided here against your actual contract with ServiceNow.

Service Now does not charge you a license for your callers (those users that your Servicedesk supports). Callers can have a user account in ServiceNow and log in with it to view their own tickets.

Managers and supervisors who receive approval requests from ServiceNow require an approver license, if they are expected to approve (or reject) requests on their own.

A full fulfiller subscription is required for every member of your support teams such as those in the Servicedesk or in the Network team managing ticket queues on ServiceNow. A user assigned a fulfiller license (like itil or contract_admin, for example), could also have other roles assigned to them (e.g., report_admin) and still count as a single fulfiller license. They can also approve (or reject) requests without being counted as an "approver" license.

From a licenses management perspective this means that you need to be careful about:

1. The total number of users accounts in your ServiceNow instance;

2. The number of users to whom an access role is granted, either individually or through membership in a group;

3. Who from your end users you want to be able to approve requests "automatically," and if those will count as an approver license.

"Automatically" is in quotes because even without assigning the approver_user role to an end-user, you could still send approval requests from ServiceNow. You could then collect the approval from the user by other means and have the support agent record the approval manually. To avoid this hassle, you need an approver license.

LDAP and licenses

Since there is no license fee for users without a role, having all of your organization as users in ServiceNow through LDAP will not increase your costs. It's free.

You should however be careful with the user groups to which you assign roles. Unless each member of your department needs to log into ServiceNow and manage ticket queues, they should not be in a privileged group in ServiceNow. Only the people actively managing ticket queues warrant such a licensing expense.

If you sync group memberships with ServiceNow, you will have a bit of a problem here. If access roles are attached to groups and are assigned automatically through membership in the group then the access role will be shared with both active and inactive members of the group. You have a couple options to deal with the situation:

Bucket groups

Create bucket groups in ServiceNow and associate access roles to those buckets. Then add and remove members to grant and revoke from them access roles (and thus licenses).

For example, you can have a Support-people group that grants its members the ITIL role and for example the report_group role. You could also have another Support-supervisors group that grants some additional roles. As usage of the application evolves, you can create new bucket groups such as Automatic-approvers, Vendors, Asset-Custodians, etc.

In this manner you continue to have your official groups managed in LDAP but also control which access roles are granted to whom consistently in ServiceNow.

Routine scripts

Periodically run scripts that revoke access roles from inactive members regardless of what the access roles the group membership conferred to the user.

For each user in ServiceNow you can know when it was the last time that they logged into ServiceNow. It would be wise to regularly check for privileged users that have not logged in for a while and consider revoking their privileged access.

Prior to the Eureka release you were able to check on the number of licensed users in your instance. A Subscription Management application was introduced in later editions[2] but you may still have to check with your ServiceNow sales representative to perform an audit. You can however get an accurate prediction by listing all unique users with a not-empty access role.

To access this list in ServiceNow look up User Roles in the Navigator, filter out users with empty roles (or with just the snc_internal role) and then group the list by users to get a unique count of the users with a role (Figure 3-6).

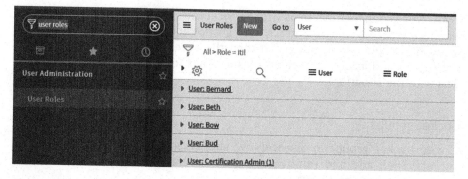

Figure 3-6. Count of all users with the itil role assigned.

Vendors access

Your Servicedesk will undoubtedly be dealing with external vendors for certain issues. Which ticketing system will you use to track dealings that involve external vendors?

Many vendors like ServiceNow will have their own ticketing system and will expect you to log a ticket through it. But if you have sufficient leverage over your vendors or they themselves don't use a ticketing system, you may get them to collaborate on tickets in your ServiceNow instance. This is what Dr. Matthias Egelhaaf from Siemens said they do with their vendors.[3]

Before giving vendors access to manage tickets in your instance consider if it would be enough for them to update tickets via email without actually being able to log into the instance with the ITIL role.

---

[2]https://docs.servicenow.com/bundle/helsinki-servicenow-platform/page/administer/subscription-management/concept/c_SubscriptionUsage.html
[3]https://www.youtube.com/watch?v=Z1Tn5LrT8NI

This is because if you give vendors the same access as other teams in your organization, they will by default be able to view and update any ticket in your instance, which could constitute a significant breach of confidentiality of your organization's day-to-day internal affairs (more on confidentiality in Chapter 9).

If it's enough for them to receive and update tickets in which they are mentioned then this is easily achievable in ServiceNow without granting your vendors any privileged role to your instance.

At its simplest, all you have to do is add their email address to the ticket watch list so that they receive notifications for the ticket and can update it by replying over email. They could also log in but as users without any role and so could only view the tickets in which they have been listed. The level of access that you give to your vendors depends on the support expectations that you have from them.

When you consult certain vendors about an issue, the responsibility for the ticket before your customer remains with the internal team that escalated the ticket. In such cases, the ticket should remain assigned to the team, which will be responsible to chase the vendor for support or find a solution through other means.

In such cases it would be sufficient if the vendor is white-listed to reply to updates via email (see Figure 3-7).

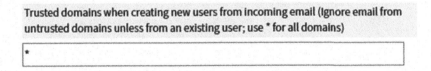

Figure 3-7. Property to list the email domains of your vendors from which you want to acccept emails in ServiceNow.

In other cases, the vendor is expected to take more responsibility for the escalated ticket and resolve it in a timely manner, directly updating the caller of the ticket (who for such issues may be from within the Technology department).

Such is normally the case with external development partners or outsource service providers who are almost considered an extension of the internal support organization. In those cases it makes sense to have the vendors as a support team to which tickets can be assigned.

In this case you need to give them more than end-user access but you should also restrict their access from seeing all tickets in your system. This is not supported by ServiceNow out-of-box and will have to be customized.

Alternatively, if you implement access on a need-to-know basis as described in Chapter 9 it will restrict access to other team's tickets and so you could safely grant vendors the same access as other fulfiller teams in your organization.

Tweet-ready takeaways

- LDAP lets an application like ServiceNow access users profiles in your organization's directory server.

- LDAP users tend to be segregated in OUs that normally represent a location or department. Use that to set users' locations in ServiceNow.

- Don't use the username to identify and match profiles; Match profiles based on an immutable ID in your LDAP server (e.g., the objectSID).

Email support

Why open tickets automatically from email and how to do it without disappointing customers

> *If you want to drive retention and repeat usage, there isn't a better way to do it than email.*
>
> —Fred Wilson,[1] Co-founder of Union Square Ventures

The quickest way to hook ServiceNow in the everyday workflows of your organization is to let ServiceNow receive emails and automatically convert them into ServiceNow tickets. This frictionless approach works even if you hope to eliminate email one day (Chapter 10).

Recognizing the power of email, every ServiceNow instance comes with an an email address built into it. If you send an email to this email address it will automatically open a ticket in ServiceNow. But telling everyone at your organization "Please email something4593@service-now.com" (your instance email address) would sure be confusing to most people who would not expect that to contact their service desk three feet away they should instead contact an external email address.

---

[1] http://avc.com/2011/05/social-medias-secret-weapon-email/

© Gabriele Kahlout 2017
G. Kahlout, *Spinning Up ServiceNow*, DOI 10.1007/978-1-4842-2571-4_4

In this chapter:

1. Tickets creation via email: An overview of the different options you have to auto-create and assign tickets in ServiceNow from email.

2. Email issues: Deal with issues that arise processing email replies to tickets, spam, and legal disclaimers.

Email address

Every ServiceNow instance comes out of the box with a built-in email address.

You could also configure ServiceNow to connect to your email servers to use your own email address for incoming emails be it directly through the support email address communicated to your organization or a new email address dedicated to ServiceNow.

But by configuring your own email address in ServiceNow you also introduce connectivity issues between your email servers and ServiceNow and the need to update your email settings in ServiceNow.

Creation options

You have a couple of options for how to create tickets in ServiceNow with varying degrees of automation.

To also auto-assign the created tickets based on the sender's location or the email address that they sent to, refer to the full discussion in Chapter 11.

Option 1: Forward emails

Simply forwarding emails to your ServiceNow email address may be the simplest option but ServiceNow will receive the email as sent from the person that forwarded it.

This means the original sender for the ticket will not be recorded as the caller of the ticket and will not receive a notification about it until a Servicedesk agent modifies the ticket and provides an update.

Option 2: Redirect emails

Unlike forwarding, with mailbox redirection emails are automatically trans-ferred as-is from one email mailbox to another.

Mailbox redirection can be set by your email administrator and doesn't require sharing of passwords nor any change in ServiceNow. Here is how it works:

1. End-users send support emails to your official support email address (e.g. helpdesk@your.org).

2. Your email server receives the emails sent to the help-desk and redirects them to your ServiceNow's instance email.

3. ServiceNow receives the emails sent from the end users as if they were sent directly to ServiceNow and creates new tickets on behalf of the senders.

This simple solution strikes through most requirements, letting you leverage the benefits of using ServiceNow's built-in instance email and also not change the email address that you have communicated to your end users. You can also:

- Configure your mailbox to keep a backup copy of each email received before redirecting it to ServiceNow;

- Set up filters in your mailbox so that emails that match certain conditions are not redirected to ServiceNow.

Also, if you have more than one support email addresses that you would like to receive as tickets in ServiceNow (e.g., helpdesk-abc@your.org and helpdesk-xyz@your.org) you can set up mailbox redirection on them also so that they too automatically redirect all incoming emails to ServiceNow.

At Al Jazeera, the teams in New York, London, and Instanbul had their mail-boxes automatically redirected to ServiceNow as described above. For the Servicedesk team in Doha however we had to devise another setup.

Option 3: Drag and drop emails

Despite the possibility of filtering out emails with specific filters both in your email mailbox and in ServiceNow some teams resist the idea of having all their emails automatically redirected to ServiceNow.

They want to manually pick which emails end up in ServiceNow and which to keep in their inbox. Once they decide that a certain email should become a ticket in ServiceNow you can have the ticket automatically created in ServiceNow by simply moving the email to a folder in their mailbox dedicated to ServiceNow. Here is how it works:

1. Create a new email address (e.g., ServiceNow@your.org) and on it set up automatic mailbox redirection as described in Option 2.

2. Make the mailbox visible with write-only access and add it as an additional mailbox for your team.

3. To create a ticket in ServiceNow from a received email drag and drop the email into the additional mailbox in your email client.

4. Once dropped into the mailbox it will be immediately redirected to ServiceNow and a ticket will be created.

Unlike forwarding emails (Option 1) moving emails to the mail folder that redirects email to ServiceNow will preserve the email headers and so ServiceNow will log the ticket as if it were sent from the caller directly.

Option 4: Manually log tickets in ServiceNow

If none of the above options work for your Servicedesk they are basically left to logging tickets on their own in ServiceNow. But then there is the risk that tickets are not logged in at all because of the additional manual labor involved in logging.

As so many ITSM champions will testify many teams start out excited about adopting the best service management practices and using ServiceNow only for that initial enthusiasm to fade away with time and people sticking with what they are already used to.

Having emails automatically redirected for them can be critical to ensure sustained commitment to using ServiceNow.

Loggging tickets manually about received emails also introduces human error where information and attachments in the received email are lost in translation and are not included in the ticket opened. Tickets may also be logged some time later.

At Al Jazeera most teams have their support email addresses automatically redirect emails to ServiceNow (Option 2) while the Servicedesk in Doha logs tickets manually (Option 4) or uses the drag and drop option (Option 3).

An increasing number of end users now also log tickets through the portal (Chapter 6) but it would be an overstatement to say that many do it.

Replies and duplicates

Now that you get emails in ServiceNow there are three common issues that you may experience from the start:

1. Uncropped email chains: Email chains are not cut out and so each update includes the whole ticket chain. It soon grows unbearable.

2. Email replies to internal notifications are shared with your end user possibly causing embarrassment.

3. Somehow, seven new tickets are created for the same issue resulting in chaos and confusion.

Reply chains

When receiving an email reply ServiceNow attempts to extract the reply part leaving out the email trail. But this may not work with your email client especially if dealing with international customers and does not work with legal disclaimers often appended to corporate emails.

If not dealt with, your ticket message details become easily unreadable and practically threaten the adoption of ServiceNow. It just becomes too ugly to deal with the ticket both over email and in the ticket itself.

To deal with this, ServiceNow lets you define what text, if found, will be cropped in an incoming email reply. You can add your disclaimer in there as well as the reply separators used in the emails that you receive. By default, ServiceNow looks for the following text strings:

-----Original Message-----

_____

From:

You may have also noticed that in the emails that you receive from the customer service of online websites you will often see that they start with something like:

In replies all text above this line is added to the ticket

They do this so that they can always crop email replies to their tickets regardless of the email client or language of the customer. You may be in a situation where such a solution suits you as well.

At Al Jazeera we have an automatic email signature (Figure 4-1) and legal disclaimer appended to every email sent, and in ServiceNow we crop email chains from the signature onwards.

Technology Planning & Governance Dir.
Technology & Network Operations Division

ALJAZEERA MEDIA NETWORK

P.O BOX 23123 DOHA, QATAR
www.aljazeera.net

This email communication is confidential and may be privileged or otherwise protected. It is intended exclusively for th
authorised to receive it. You should not copy or disclose its contents to anyone. If you are not such an intended recipie
attachments and destroy any copies of it. We regret any inconvenience resulting from erroneous delivery of this mess:
Please note that none of the AlJazeera Media Network or any of its affiliated entities will have any liability for any incor
Emails are not secure and cannot be guaranteed to be error free. Anyone who communicates with us by email is take:
do not necessarily represent those of the AlJazeera Media Network or any of its affiliated entities. Any logo trademark
AlJazeera Media Network. Any unauthorized reproduction copying or other use by you or others is strictly prohibited.

Figure 4-1. Email signature and disclaimer automatically appended to outgoing emails from Al Jazeera.

Reply duplicates

As tickets started to pour in automatically in ServiceNow from emails sent by unassuming colleagues all over the channel at Al Jazeera we soon observed an issue: people were receiving duplicate copies of the same ticket. It seemed like every new email reply received spawned a new ticket instead of updating the first one.

Upon investigation we realized what the issue was: Reply all. Reply-alls to the original email that was sent to ServiceNow triggered new tickets. Here is how it can happen for you as well:

1. The service desk email address redirects to ServiceNow automatically.

2. Carla emails the service desk and her line manager Imad with a support request.

3. ServiceNow automatically opens a ticket for Carla's email and emails her a receipt notice.

4. Imad replies to Carla's email and to the service desk (reply all).

5. ServiceNow receives Imad's email. Eventhough the email is a reply there is no ticket number mentioned in the email and so ServiceNow opens a new ticket for Imad.

6. The issue repeats with each reply to the service desk email address but doesn't have a ticket number in the email trail.

So unless the email is a reply to a ServiceNow notification the email will be processed in ServiceNow as a new Incident ticket generating many confusing duplicate tickets and notifications.

From a system perspective it makes sense. How could ServiceNow tell if the new email is a reply to an existing ticket or a new ticket if there is no ticket number in it?

To deal with the issue you could go in either of these two directions:

1. Ignore email replies that don't contain a ticket number. This way Imad's message would be received by Carla but wouldn't reflect in ServiceNow and won't trigger any duplicate email.

2. Attempt to match email subject lines with the short description of open tickets.

Ignoring the email reply may not be sensible unless you also include a mechanism for the service desk to review those ignored email replies (there may be an approval or instruction for the service desk). You could tie this in with the Feedback list mentioned later in this chapter.

You could also send an auto-reply to Imad alerting him that because he replied to an email without a ticket number the email was ignored and invite him to email again in a new email instead if he wants to communicate with the service desk. But that's just too cumbersome and confusing, isn't it?

At Al Jazeera we went with the second option so that even email replies that don't contain a ticket number will update the most recent open ticket as long as the following conditions match:

1. The ticket has the same short description as the subject line of the email reply (after trimming reply prefixes and trailining spaces).

2. The sender of the email or at least one of the people to whom the email is also sent is also in the ticket's watch list. In other words, the email and the ticket have at least one person in common.

3. If there is more than one ticket matching the above criteria, update the most recently updated open ticket.

This solution only comes into play after ServiceNow's default workflow gives up on processing the incoming email as a ticket update. So it doesn't impact the reply's processing logic. It does however place itself before the logic for creating new incidents.

If you also implement this, carefully test the creation of new incidents from email and monitor that no reply ends up matching wrong tickets.

This procedure has been in place at Al Jazeera for years and works as expected. It doesn't solve the issue entirely, especially when email groups are involved and so a common denominator is not found (second condition). But for most cases updating the right ticket instead of creating new tickets works. When it fails it creates a new ticket, which would have happened anyway.

To be sure that emails are not incorrectly matched with other tickets that have the same subject line (e.g., "I need help"), you could also either:

• Record the first short description set for a ticket in a hidden field so that even if the service desk changes the short description of the ticket, the matching will occur against the original subject line the ticket was created with. We do this at Al Jazeera.

• Make a ticket's short description unchangeable. As it was received so it remains.

Missed replies

When a new ticket is received ServiceNow will trigger a notification about the new ticket (see Chapter 5) but until the ticket is assigned to someone any further update by the caller will not trigger any notification to anyone. The customer updates will be silently posted to the ticket with no one alerted.

This may be ideal in theory, assuming teams regularly check their tickets queue and process each ticket in it diligently. In practice however it can lead to certain ticket updates being missed for some time and growing customer dissatisfaction.

This is even more so in the beginning when teams may have officially been on-boarded to ServiceNow but in reality they still have not entirely shifted their workflows. In such cases it is even more likely that unless new email notifications are received tickets will remain neglected in ServiceNow.

To avoid this situation at least as teams get accustomed to checking and processing tickets in ServiceNow you may establish that every new ticket update made by a customer is in turn delivered to someone to take care of.

At Al Jazeera, until the ticket is assigned to an individual new customer updates are shared with the entire assignment group of the ticket. This is to prompt someone from the team to assign the ticket and reply to the customer.

I've also been told of other ServiceNow customers that instead of delivering the customer update to the to the entire group they deliver it to the group's manager.

Thank you issue

When our central Servicedesk at Al Jazeera shifted to ServiceNow a funny and totally unexpected issue got continuously reported and came to be known as the "thank you issue"!

As said above if a customer writes an update to a ticket a notification would only be delivered to the assignee.

But in many cases the assigneen would have left for the shift and so the only way to know about the update would be an angry call from the customer wondering why it is taking so long to process her update normally to a marked-resolved ticket.

So the following workflow was introduced:

1. Email replies to resolved tickets are shown as *feedback* in a special home page gauge visible to the service desk.

2. The service desk reviews the latest customer message on the ticket and based on it either:

    •   Re-opens the ticket and resets the assignment as appropriate in the current shift or

    •   Marks the ticket's feedback as *noted* to clear it from the list.

This feedback list on the ServiceNow home page (Figure 4-2) made sure our service desk was on top of all ticket replies to closed tickets from customer, regardless of the team the ticket was assigned to.

Figure 4-2. Feedback list on the service desk home page shows resolved tickets to which new comments have been added.

This allowed the service desk to help ensure appropriate action is taken to all customer messages.

As a side note, the reason this became known as the Thank you issue was because we had set every reply to a closed ticket to automatically re-open the ticket and also re-assign it to the service desk, who in turn would assign the ticket after checking the availability and load of support teams on shift.

In the beginning the Servicedesk was the only team fully-vested in ServiceNow and so to maintain operational fluency additional oversight was needed from service desk over the tickets assigned to other teams.

But this soon led to the issue that came to be known as the Thank you issue. So many times customers would reply to the closure notification, re-opening the ticket with "Thank you"! It would happen like this:

- Service desk writes a message and resolves the ticket.

- Caller and others in the watch list receive the notification.

- Caller replies to the received message with "Thank you."

- The ticket is automatically re-opened with the received message.

- In order to close the ticket the service desk has to write another message.

- Prompted by the caller's thank you, others in the watch list also post their thank you reply, again re-opening the ticket!

This funny situation kept on happening so often until we introduced the feedback list solution described above.

Internal replies

ServiceNow by default processes email replies to ticket notifications and posts all of them to the user-visible ticket comments. This in turn triggers the appropriate notifications for the agents or the end users (depending on who wrote the update).

But this processes also applies to email replies to internal notifications such as *Assigned to me* and *Assigned to your group*.

To avoid internal recipients from replying to those emails with internal replies (like "Why did I get this assigned?") you could include a warning in the email notifications clarifying that replies will be sent to the caller directly (not to the person that just made the assignment).

Alternatively you may want to enable an internal communication thread for each ticket. As such email replies to assignment emails are posted to the ticket's work notes and are not customer-visible. This is discussed in context in Chapter 10.

Filter out spam

Once email processing is enabled in ServiceNow external spammers may find out and start sending spam emails to your instance which in turn will auto-create tickets and trigger email notifications.

You can avoid this by whitelisting emails from friendly domains only as well as whitelisting individual private email addresses that are explicitly added to the watch list by a member of staff. Here is how it would work:

1. In order to process a ticket, HR or the service desk may need to communicate with an external private email address (e.g., an @gmail.com address). This may be for example when interviewing or on-boarding a new candidate employee. The email address could also be that of an external collaborator that the network team needs to consult on a particular ticket.

2. The external email address is added to the ticket's watch list as an email address. This automatically white lists incoming emails from this particular email address.

Your ServiceNow administrator can also whitelist entire domains, for example those of your vendors and partners (e.g., @ibm.com) through a dedicated property in ServiceNow.

Whitelisting at both the individual level and the domain level works fine for Al Jazeera's needs and may also for your organization.

But if you need to receive emails from domains and addresses that cannot be specified a priori whatsoever, whitelisting won't work for you. You can alternatively rely on SPAM Scoring[2] and check your ServiceNow Junk folder often.

Just like SPAM is filtered out by email servers ServiceNow's SPAM scoring plug-in will analyze incoming emails and assess the likelihood of the email being spam based on ServiceNow's experience.

Based on the SPAM score assigned by ServiceNow to the incoming email you can decide whether to ignore the email or let it through as a legitimate email.

ServiceNow lets you set the SPAM score that you are willing to tolerate as legitimate; Setting a low score means that you will ignore most emails potentially considered as spam and let in only those that don't look suspicious. This means you potentially may miss legitimate emails that were scored as suspicious. By contrast a high tolerance score for SPAM will let in emails that were highly suspected of being spam.

In the next chapter we also review how to ensure that you do not send out spam.

Tweet-ready take aways

- The quickest way to hook ServiceNow in the everyday workflows of your organization is to automatically create tickets from emails.

- Mailbox redirection can be set by your email administrator and doesn't require sharing of passwords nor any change in ServiceNow.

- Emails from customer service often start with something like: ## In replies all text above this line is added to the ticket ##

- A feedback list on the home page helps make sure the service desk is on top of all ticket replies to closed tickets from customers.

---

[2]https://hi.service-now.com/kb_view.do?sysparm_article=KB0549426

Elegant Notifications

Why robotic email notifications are not how you want your customers to perceive you

This chapter is about the email notifications sent from ServiceNow, which for many people at your organization and especially those in management positions is all they get to see of your ITSM and ServiceNow programs.

ServiceNow comes ready out of box (OOB) to receive and to send email notifications but even though the OOB notifications sent from ServiceNow are now better than they used to be in earlier versions they are still too terse and uninformative. At least the notifications sent to your end users should be branded and aesthetically pleasing in order to convey a better image of your team.

The OOB notifications basically just push the recipient to go to ServiceNow to find out more and act on the notification. Technical people may be sympathetic to such style but other recipients not having the patience to go through the ticket's web interface may find it an annoying delay to progress on tickets and seek support through other means (e.g., an escalation). They are your customers and they know it.

© Gabriele Kahlout 2017

G. Kahlout, *Spinning Up ServiceNow*, DOI 10.1007/978-1-4842-2571-4_5

If your ServiceNow instance is accessible only behind a VPN (as it is at Al Jazeera for example) it will be even more difficult for users to log into ServiceNow from their mobile device. It becomes imperative that your notifications contain sufficient guidance on what is needed from the recipients and that they can provide it without leaving thier inbox.

Taking customer-facing notifications seriously at Al Jazeera, before we went live with ServiceNow in Doha each notification was reviewed by our Chief Technology Officer. This chapter helps you do the same, offering corresponding examples from Al Jazeera and others so that you can customize to your liking the number and content of the notifications sent from your instance to your users.

In this chapter I also warn against spam emails. It has happened with us at Al Jazeera and it made a headline when it also happened at the UK's National Health Service (NHS) spamming 840,000 employees at once.[1]

In this chapter:

- Customer-facing notifications: How many there are per ticket and how they look;

- Internal notifications;
  Spam: It can happen that the system will spam customers and the organization en masse. Understand how and prevent this blunder from happening.

Robotic content

Even though people tend not to admit it or downplay it consumer behavior studies and even brain scans have confirmed that the packaging of a product influences our perception of the product itself.

Coke drunk from a red can tastes sweeter than the same formula Coke in a white-colored can, and a strawberry mousse tastes sweeter if served in a white container than if served from a black one.[2]

If you think about it it for a moment this is a remarkable finding with profound implications. As technologists we tend to shun the role of aesthetics in our systems as an afterthought. That's a pity because as Steve Jobs understood "some people think design means how it looks. But of course, if you dig deeper, it's really how it works!"

---

[1]http://www.telegraph.co.uk/news/2016/11/14/nhs-it-blunder-sees-system-clogged-after-email-sent-to-12-millio/
[2]http://www.packagingdigest.com/packaging-design/the-truth-about-how-food-packaging-influences-taste-perception-2016-02-02

What this means for digital products and services is that the aesthetic look of digital screens that you present yourself with to your customers influences their perception of your services. The more elegant and professional the emails you send, the better the image of your support organization will be in the minds of your colleagues.

President Barack Obama has been cited for using this understanding to great profit in his 2012 re-election campaign.[3] The campaign which raised $690 million dollars online mostly from fundraising emails employed a team of 20 writers and a sophisticated analytics system to measure and improve those emails.

I'm not asking that you go that far for your ServiceNow emails but consider these guidelines:

- Use copy that is customer-centric and in simple language, leaving out IT and ITIL jargon.

- Use subject lines that are descriptive and consistent.

- Clarify why the recipient is receiving the email notification and what action is required from her.

- Enable recipients to act upon emails directly via email and on the go without having to leave their email inbox.

- Brand customer-facing email notifications to portray a professional and caring image of your support team.

The wording and layout of ServiceNow's default notifications sent to customers is somewhat robotic (see Figure 5-3) while nowadays end users are getting accustomed to much more natural and customer-centric language in notifications and error messages, as can be seen in Figures 5-1 and 5-2.

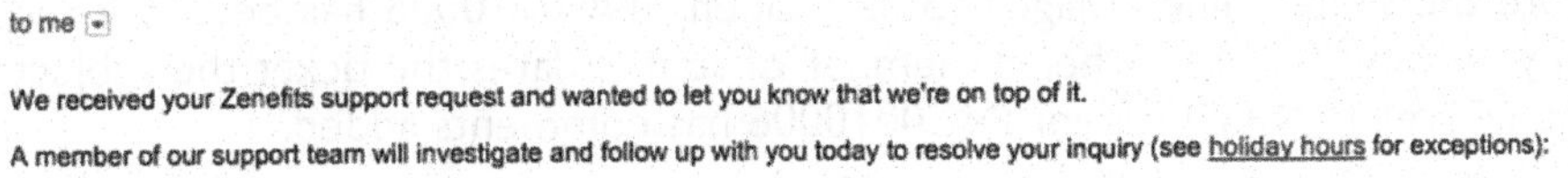

to me ▾

We received your Zenefits support request and wanted to let you know that we're on top of it.

A member of our support team will investigate and follow up with you today to resolve your inquiry (see holiday hours for exceptions):

Figure 5-1. Auto-responder emails do not have to read robotic. They can tell the recipient that you are "on top of it."

---

[3]http://www.theatlantic.com/technology/archive/2012/11/hey-i-need-to-talk-to-you-about-this-brilliant-obama-email-scheme/265725/

Thanks for writing in!

We can't wait to help out and will get back to you faster than it takes Kanye to jump on stage at the Grammys.

Our normal hours are 9am–6pm PST Monday–Friday, but please check out our Help Center for answers to our most frequently asked questions.

Cheers,
The Titer Happiness Team

Figure 5-2. Auto-responder emails can be informative and set the expectations for your reply time frame.

 IT Service Desk to me ⌄

INC0010006 - VPN not working

An incident has been opened on your behalf.

You can view all the details of the incident by following the link below:

Take me to the Incident

Thank you.

Ref:MSG0000032

Figure 5-3. ServiceNow out-of-box notification sent to the caller when the ticket is logged.

Note the subject line in Figure 5-3, "Incident INC0010006 has been opened on your behalf". "And when a member of staff updates the ticket the subject line will read, "Your Incident INC0010006 has comments added."

Note how odd such email subjects look in the inbox when compared to normal email conversations people engage in. Do they need to be this way?

At the Obama campaign they found that "the subject lines that worked best were things you might see in your in-box from other people."

Just because you now have an ITSM ticketing system your service desk subject lines don't suddenly have to turn robotic.

Customer-facing notifications

Here is a review of the email notification templates sent by ServiceNow to the caller of an incident until it's resolved and after:

1. Incident opened notification: Sent to the caller as a receipt as soon as the Incident is logged.

2. Incident commented: Sent when your support agent leaves a new update on the Incident ticket.

3. Incident requires action: Sent when your support agent marks the Incident as requiring customer action.

4. Incident resolved: Sent when the Incident is marked as resolved.

5. Incident closed: Another notification sent 24 hours after the Incident is resolved.

All of those notifications to the customer are too many and reflect too much the internal life cycle of an Incident.

1. Incident opened receipt

The "incident opened for me" notification as it's called in ServiceNow is an automatic reply sent to the caller of an incident as soon as the incident is received (Figure 5-4).

It is like a receipt providing the caller with evidence of her contact, setting expectations and providing details for further reference to the issue (Figure 5-5).

 IT Service Desk to me ⭥

INC0010006 - VPN not working

An incident has been opened on your behalf.

You can view all the details of the incident by following the link below:

Take me to the Incident

Thank you.

Ref:MSG0000032

Figure 5-4. Out-of-box incident opened notification

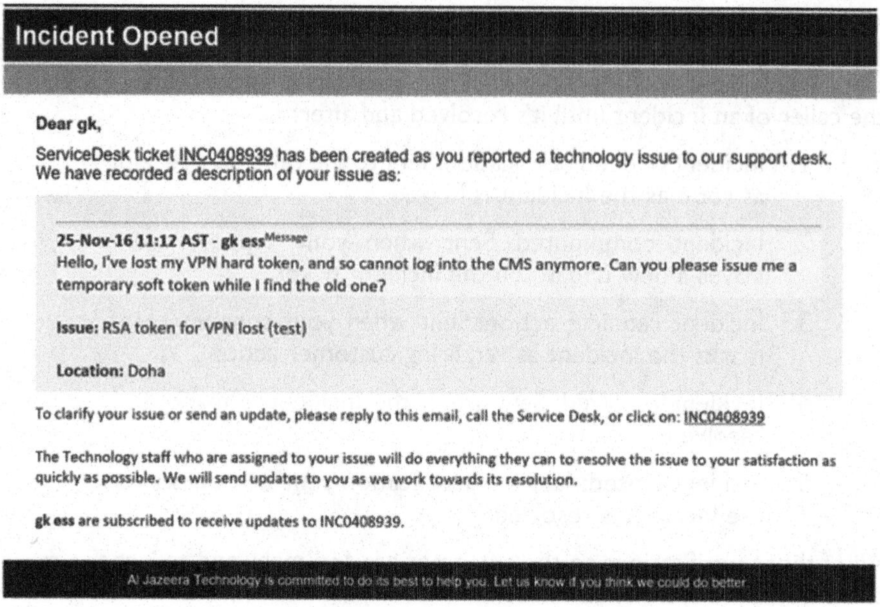

Incident Opened

Dear gk,

ServiceDesk ticket INC0408939 has been created as you reported a technology issue to our support desk. We have recorded a description of your issue as:

25-Nov-16 11:12 AST - gk ess^Message

Hello, I've lost my VPN hard token, and so cannot log into the CMS anymore. Can you please issue me a temporary soft token while I find the old one?

Issue: RSA token for VPN lost (test)

Location: Doha

To clarify your issue or send an update, please reply to this email, call the Service Desk, or click on: INC0408939

The Technology staff who are assigned to your issue will do everything they can to resolve the issue to your satisfaction as quickly as possible. We will send updates to you as we work towards its resolution.

gk ess are subscribed to receive updates to INC0408939.

Al Jazeera Technology is committed to do its best to help you. Let us know if you think we could do better

Figure 5-5. Incident opened notification at Al Jazeera.

The branded notification above features:

- A personal greeting to the recipient;

- Commitment from the Technology service desk to solve the issue, and to the best possible standard;

- Clarification as to how the customer can update the ticket, that nothing yet is currently expected from her, and that she will be receiving updates.

As for the subject line the default one in ServiceNow reads:

Incident INC0000011 – opened on your behalf

Looking through your inbox it's difficult to tell what this INC000011 was about. The subject line could be more descriptive and natural than this. For example at Al Jazeera it's like this:

OPENED: VPN is not working – INC0000011

"VPN is not working" is the short description of the Incident. Instead of OPENED you could also say "RECEIVED" for example. Or you could make it really natural and conversational and have this subject line for all ticket notifications:

RE:VPN is not working

2. Incident comments updated

When there is a reply on the ticket a new notification is sent to the caller with the update. Figure 5-6 is how the incident commented notification looks out of the box while Figure 5-7 shows how it has been customized at Al Jazeera.

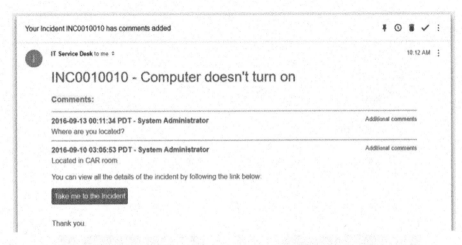

Figure 5-6. Out-of-box notification sent when there is an update to the ticket.

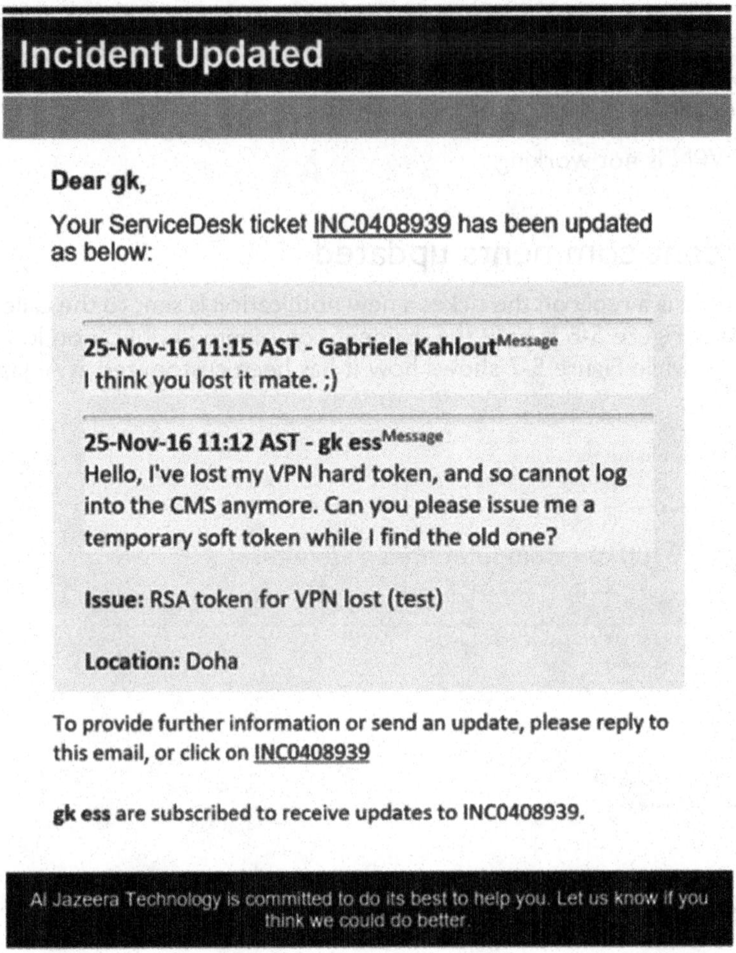

Incident Updated

Dear gk,

Your ServiceDesk ticket INC0408939 has been updated as below:

25-Nov-16 11:15 AST - Gabriele Kahlout[Message]
I think you lost it mate. ;)

25-Nov-16 11:12 AST - gk ess[Message]
Hello, I've lost my VPN hard token, and so cannot log into the CMS anymore. Can you please issue me a temporary soft token while I find the old one?

Issue: RSA token for VPN lost (test)

Location: Doha

To provide further information or send an update, please reply to this email, or click on INC0408939

gk ess are subscribed to receive updates to INC0408939.

Al Jazeera Technology is committed to do its best to help you. Let us know if you think we could do better.

Figure 5-7. Incident updated notification is triggered when a message is added to the support conversation with the caller.

For the subject line this is the default subject line:

Your Incident INC0000011 – has comments added

Much more descriptive and natural would be either of:

UPDATED:VPN is not working – INC0000011

RE:VPN is not working

3. Action required

As noted earlier ServiceNow default subject lines do little in attracting the recipient's attention.

When the service desk cannot proceed with the resolution of a ticket because it requires further input from the caller, their approval to a suggested solution, or their availability in person the service desk can change the state of a ticket to On hold, awaiting caller.

To make this clear to the caller it is better to use a subject line that indicates the need for action as also done by Amazon.com (see Figure 5-8) for example.

Figure 5-8. The subject lines of emails that require customer intervention commonly include "Action Required".

Inside the Action Required email, clarify that you are waiting for further input from the customer before you can proceed with the ticket (see Figure 5-9).

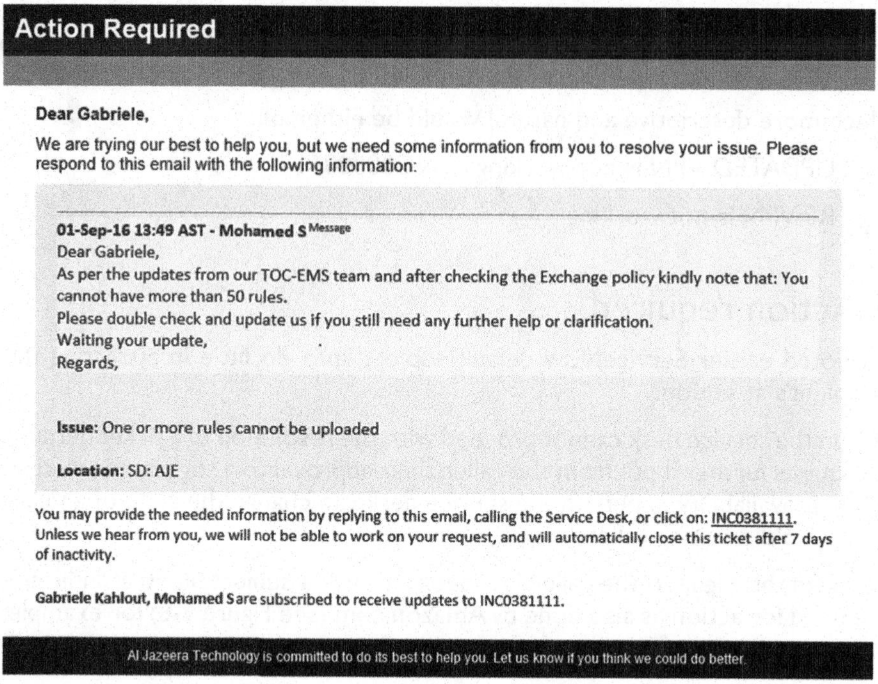

Action Required

Dear Gabriele,

We are trying our best to help you, but we need some information from you to resolve your issue. Please respond to this email with the following information:

01-Sep-16 13:49 AST - Mohamed S Message
Dear Gabriele,
As per the updates from our TOC-EMS team and after checking the Exchange policy kindly note that: You cannot have more than 50 rules.
Please double check and update us if you still need any further help or clarification.
Waiting your update,
Regards,

Issue: One or more rules cannot be uploaded

Location: SD: AJE

You may provide the needed information by replying to this email, calling the Service Desk, or click on: INC0381111.
Unless we hear from you, we will not be able to work on your request, and will automatically close this ticket after 7 days of inactivity.

Gabriele Kahlout, Mohamed S are subscribed to receive updates to INC0381111.

Al Jazeera Technology is committed to do its best to help you. Let us know if you think we could do better.

Figure 5-9. Action Required email clearly informs the caller that you are no longer working on the ticket, waiting for feedback.

Just like it is mandatory to leave a comment to the caller when resolving an Incident it should be the case also when putting a ticket on hold so that callers know what is requested of them exactly.

4. Incident resolved

The incident resolved notification (see Figures 5-10, 5-11 and 5-12) is sent to the caller once the incident is resolved. It is also an opportunity to:

- Show commitment to full satisfaction of the caller;
- Provide guidance on how to re-open the case or provide feedback.

Incident Closed

Dear Gabriele,

We want to let you know that your ticket <u>INC0386856</u> has been closed as described below:

22-Sep-16 13:13 AST - Khaled M I ^{Message}

This is to confirm that the issue has been resolved after typing the username and password since we are using local account.

Please let us know if you require any further assistance.
Best regards.

Issue: no internet connection

Location: SD: AJE

NOT FULLY SATISFIED?

To reopen this ticket click on the following link and it will open a new email window; Describe your issue and click on Send.

<u>REOPEN INC0386856</u>

<u>PROVIDE FEEDBACK INC0386856</u>

Gabriele Kahlout, Khaled M I are subscribed to receive updates to INC0386856.

Al Jazeera Technology is committed to do its best to help you. Let us know if you think we could do better.

Figure 5-10. *Incident resolved notification sent at Al Jazeera.*

* Additional comments (Customer visible)	I
	Comments are required when resolving an Incident

Figure 5-11. *To resolve an Incident one must first type a comment.*

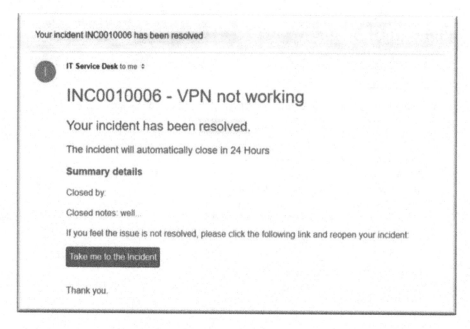

Figure 5-12. Out-of-box incident resolved notification.

In the Al Jazeera notification of Figure 5-11 you will notice that the notification doesn't distinguish between resolved and closed. This is because we only send one email notification once the email is resolved and have disabled the incident closed notifications sent automatically 24 hours after the Incident is resolved.

The customer does not need to be bothered about the ITIL difference between a resolved and a closed incident. This state transition does not need to trigger an email notification to anyone since no action is required.

In fact you could even disable the incident resolved notification to make the experience with the ticket more like a natural conversation that dies off with both parties going quiet as opposed to one explicitly announcing the termination and giving an ultimatum to respond before the ticket is "permanently closed"!

In each *Incident updated* notification sent you can still clearly indicate the status of the ticket (work in progress or resolved).

5. Incident closed

By default 24 hours after an incident has been resolved ServiceNow would send the caller another email notification (see Figure 5-13) telling her that the Incident is now closed (see Figure 5-14). First it was resolved, now it is closed.

Incident has been closed.

Summary details

Closed by: System Administrator

Closed notes: well...

You can view all the details of the incident by following the link below:

Take me to the Incident

Thank you.

Ref:MSG0000047

Figure 5-13. Incident closed notification sent automatically 24 hours after the Incident resolved notification.

| | IT Service Desk | **Your incident INC0010006 has been closed** – Incident has been closed. Summary details Closed by... |
| | IT Service Desk | **Your incident INC0010006 has been resolved** – INC0010006 - VPN not working Your incident has b... |

Figure 5-14. The first notification is about the incident resolved; the second is sent automatically after 24 hours of inactivity to notify that the incident is now also closed. Does the customer care to receive this many notifications?

Subject lines

Those were all the customer-facing notifications sent by ServiceNow. Before moving on to internal notifications Table 5-1 lists all the customer-facing notifications and proposed subject lines for each.

Table 5-1. Customer-facing email notifications

	Original email subject	Proposed email subject
New ticket	Incident INCXXXXXXX has been opened on your behalf	RECEIVED: Short description – INCXXXXXXX
Ticket updated	Your Incident INCXXXXXXX has comments added	RE: Short description – INCXXXXXXX
Action required	Your Incident INCXXXXXXX has comments added	ACTION REQUIRED: Short description – INCXXXXXXX
Ticket resolved	Your Incident INCXXXXXXX has been resolved	RESOLVED: Short description – INCXXXXXXX
Ticket closed	Your Incident INCXXXXXXX has been closed	Disable notification

Duplicates

On several occasions ServiceNow could send duplicate or unnecessary emails to your customers.

For example when a ticket is resolved your customer could potentially receive two separate notifications at the same time (Figure 5-15). One would be notifying her and others in the watch list that a comment has been added to the ticket and another that the ticket has been resolved.

Figure 5-15. If another person is listed to a watch list then when the Incident is resolved the caller may receive two duplicate notifications with the same message.

A simple and bullet-proof solution in this case would be to disable the incident resolved notification altogether so that the incident updated notification is all that gets sent.

More sophisticated solutions also exist. Because modifying the notifications workflow can be messy and lead either to undesired notifications being sent to customers or possibly important notifications never being sent, it is important that you test such changes thoroughly as discussed in Chapter 8.

Reply all

Duplicate notifications may also be generated when recipients reply all and there are multiple people watching the ticket (a very common scenario, as discussed in Chapter 10).

To avoid this reply all duplication ServiceNow can hide recipients in the BCC and list who else is subscribed to receive updates to the ticket with a line in the body of the notification. It could read like this:

> John, Bob, Alice, and IT Dept. are subscribed to receive updates to INCXXX.

At Al Jazeera we do not want customers to directly email the agent working on the ticket from the IT side as that would defeat the purpose of the system. But we do not have an issue showing their names in the ticket to make the conversation with the customer more personal.

We are in fact also considering showing a photo of the assigned-to person in the notification and encouraging the caller to provide feedback about the support she received from him. We believe this personalization of support will make the caller more sympathetic and less critical of the person providing support. Research from Twitter bears this out, and for this they rolled out a feature to shows the name and face of customer-care agents helping customers on Twitter.[4]

Internal notifications

In addition to the customer-facing email notification listed above, ServiceNow will also send internal notifications to your support team in the following four scenarios:

- Incident opened and unassigned: Sent as soon as a new ticket is received and it is not already assigned to anyone;

Yet this notification is by default not sent to anybody unless they individually subscribe to receive it.

- Incident assigned to my group: Sent to the email address of the team that the ticket has been assigned to;

- Incident assigned to me: Sent to the person to whom the incident has been assigned;

- Incident commented: Sent to the person the ticket has been assigned to as soon as the caller updates the ticket with a message. If other people have been subscribed to receive ticket updates they also will receive this notification.

Unlike with caller notifications those four internal notifications are not too many and are all actionable by the recipient (see Table 5-2). I herewith only recommend modifications to the content of the notifications and especially to the Incident commented notification as it would also end up being received by people on your customer's side.

---

[4]https://blog.twitter.com/2017/personalize-customer-experiences-in-direct-messages

Table 5-2. Internal notifications triggered for incidents

	Original email subject	Proposed email subject
New unassigned ticket	Incident INCXXXXXXX – opened and unassigned	NEW: Short description – INCXXXXXXX
Ticket assigned to group	Incident INCXXXXXXX has been assigned to group Group-Name	UNASSIGNED: Short description – INCXXXXXXX
Ticked assigned to individual	Incident INCXXXXXXX has been assigned to you	YOURS: Short description – INCXXXXXXX

At the subject line level, here are the default subject lines for each notification. Adapt them as you see fit for your team.

Also note that ServiceNow does not provide notifications for internal conversations about the ticket (see Chapter 10 for details).

1. New unassigned incident

Incidents in ServiceNow may be logged without setting an assignment group and such is the case for incidents sent over email. So who should be notified of new and unassigned Incidents?

There is an *Opened and unassigned* notification that alerts about new incidents received but by default it is not configured to be delivered to anyone. So you have four options with respect to this notification:

1. Subscribe some users to receive this notification and then assign the ticket to your service desk or another team. This option doesn't require any configuration; Users can subscribe to the notification from their profile page.

2. Modify the notification so that it's always sent to your service desk group as well as other subscribers.

3. Set tickets to be automatically assigned to the service desk, so that this notification would never be needed (or triggered).

4. Do nothing, assuming that service desk members will always be monitoring their ServiceNow home page for new tickets during hours of operation.

As for the contents of the notification, the default is not too bad and since it is an internal notification you may not need to customize it (Figure 5-16).

INC0010016 - Laptop very slooow

Additional Details:

Caller: Fred L

category: Inquiry / Help

Severity: 3 - Low

Priority: 5 - Planning

You can view all the details of the incident by following the link below:

Take me to the Incident

Thank you.

Figure 5-16. Contents of an internal notification sent about a new Incident ticket

2. Incident assigned to group

Once a ticket is re-assigned from one group to another, from the service desk to the network team for example, the team will receive a notification with the same contents as the unassigned email notification above (figure 6-18).

Identify which fields you deem important to list in the email and modify the email template accordingly. At Al Jazeera we list the following:

Location: Portacabin 2 - Doha

Priority: P2 - High (10h), SLA due by 13-Jun-16 13:17

Opened by: at 12-Jun-16 13:17

Assigned to: gk HD

Last updated by kahloutg at 12-Jun-16 13:17

State: Open

3. Incident assigned to person

This notification serves the same purpose as the *Assigned to my group* notification but is sent to the person to whom the ticket has been assigned.

4. Incident updated

This notification is very important because it will carry the email replies from the caller to the ticket.

It's sent to the assignee but also to other people subscribed to receive updates on the ticket. Those would normally be people from the caller-side such as the line manager or the entire group interested in the resolution of the ticket.

For such end user audiences the default template may be inappropriate (see Figure 5-17).

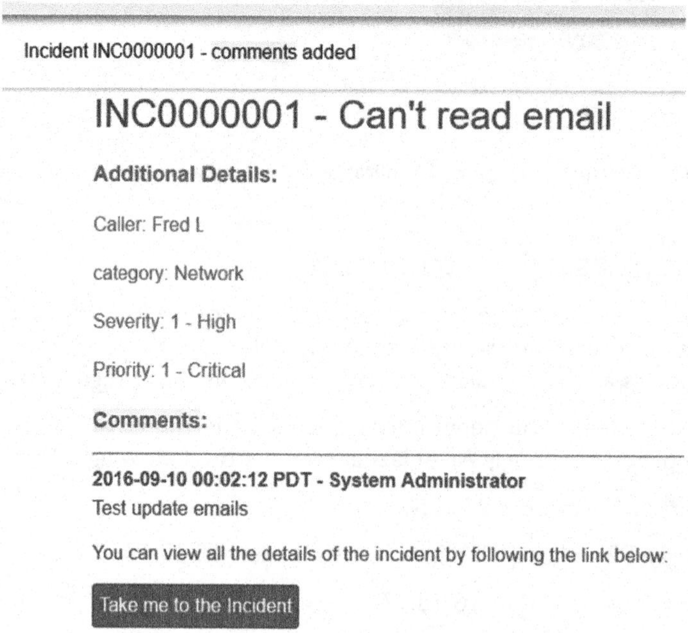

Incident INC0000001 - comments added

INC0000001 - Can't read email

Additional Details:

Caller: Fred L

category: Network

Severity: 1 - High

Priority: 1 - Critical

Comments:

2016-09-10 00:02:12 PDT - System Administrator
Test update emails

You can view all the details of the incident by following the link below:

Take me to the Incident

Figure 5-17. Out-of-box Incident commented (ITIL) notification sent to the assignee and to watch list subscribers, if any

A simple solution to this problem is to use the exact same content template and subject line used in the notification that is sent to the caller. This should avoid confusion on any side by keeping things the same on both ends of the conversation.

Another issue with this notification is that it's sent to multiple people. The problem with this is that when people hit reply all to respond to the notification the recipients will receive two email notifications.

Spam notifications

ServiceNow could potentially spam your entire organization at once!

This depends on your organization's email setup but basically could happen any time ServiceNow sends an automated notification.

For example if ServiceNow receives a notification from an all-staff group email, the auto-reply *Incident opened* notification could be automatically delivered to all staff.

It could also be triggered accidentally (or intentionally) from ServiceNow by someone adding group emails to the watch list of the ticket and triggering an update.

This is not a theoretical scenario; it happens in practice. The National Health Service (NHS) in the UK once sent the estimated total of 200 million unnecessary emails to 840,000 employees within four hours.[5]

Screenshots posted by the BBC of the email sent show that troublesome emails were sent from a service desk address.[6] On the issue Dr. Andrew Hartle from St Mary's Hospital in London commented on this by saying: "We should ban 'reply to all'—it's the bane of everyone's life."

Through a slightly different setup this once happened at Al Jazeera also and one night four incident notifications were sent to all of Al Jazeera's staff!

A notification from HR had been sent to a dynamic group that automatically included all emails at Al Jazeera. So ServiceNow also received the notification, promptly created an Incident ticket, and sent back the Incident opened notification to HR and the dynamic group with all staff. This, in turn led to a circle that generated three more ticket updated notifications.

What a disaster it was! Damage done we pulled back those emails from people's mailboxes and revisited our email configuration to prevent this from happening again. Don't wait it for it to happen to you too; ask your email and ServiceNow administrators from the outset about the measures in place to prevent mass spam from being sent in any case.

---

[5]http://www.telegraph.co.uk/news/2016/11/14/nhs-it-blunder-sees-system-clogged-after-email-sent-to-12-millio/
[6]http://www.bbc.com/news/technology-37979456

In most Microsft Exchange environments, administrators have it set up that only a few email addresses at the organization could email certain user groups and there is a limit on the total number of emails within the organization that could be emailed at once. You should verify this to be the case at your organization and confirm it will work with the email address your ServiceNow instance uses to send out emails. If this is not possible at your organization, you may implement a similar mechanism within ServiceNow.

Tweet-ready takeaways

- We tend to shun aesthetics in our systems as an afterthought but in the mind of the user looks and function are intrinsically intertwined.

- The 2012 Obama campaign found "the subject lines that worked best were things you might see in your in-box from other people."

- Just because you now have an ITSM ticketing system your service desk subject lines don't suddenly have to turn robotic.

- Emails with generic subject lines are easily passed over. It's better to indicate in the subject line that "Action is Required."

- We should ban "reply to all"—it's the bane of everyone's life. www.telegraph.co.uk/news/2016/11/14/nhs-it-blunder-sees-system-clogged-after-email-sent-to-12-millio/

- To avoid reply-all duplication, hide recipients in the BCC and list who else is subscribed to receive updates in the body of the notification.

- The customer does not need to be bothered about the ITIL difference between a resolved and a closed incident.

Request portal

How complex Request fulfillment can be and how to win with a consistent user experience

> *The only defense a person has in our over-communicated society is an oversimplified mind.*
>
> —Al Ries & Jack Trout[1]

Put simply, to an end user, IT either fixes stuff that is broken (Incident management) or provides new stuff (Request fulfillment). Which one does your department do more?

Request fulfillment is undoubtedly integral to the everyday work of any IT department. Every day there will be requests for new equipment from headsets to new workstations, requests for software installations or other services, such as new email groups, FTP folders, or yet other services that also require coordination with HR and facilities departments such as the off-boarding of terminated employees.

Other departments also handle user requests of their own such as applications for medical insurance, visitor passes, or cameramen deployments. The day-to-day work of many employees in an organization can be seen through the lenses of receiving requests from internal or external customers, and going through the motions of fulfilling them. Hence, the new buzzword Enterprise Service Management.

---

[1] Ries, Al; Trout, Jack; *Positioning: The Battle For Your Mind*, McGraw-Hill, New York, 1981, page 5.

© Gabriele Kahlout 2017
G. Kahlout, *Spinning Up ServiceNow*, DOI 10.1007/978-1-4842-2571-4_6

At the CERN particle physics lab in Switzerland, scientists, staff, and visitors can go to an online portal from which they can request IT services or rent a bicycle on-site.

Being systematic with your requests fulfillment process allows you to streamline and automate the flow of information and responsibility for the tasks involved in fulfilling a request in a consistent and trackable sequence, akin to a digital assembly line.

Unlike logging incidents however, Request fulfillment does not work by just redirecting emails from end users in ServiceNow and voila requests are created automatically in ServiceNow. For every request, there is a form to be filled, and approval and fulfillment workflows to be defined up-front.

In this chapter:

1. *Request components:* Overview of what it takes to fulfill a request in ServiceNow from both the perspective of the requester and of the fulfiller's teams

2. *World-class examples:* Examples of front-end portals and the process that went into their making

3. *Handling approvals:* What could go wrong and how to avoid management blunders

4. *Simplified collaboration:* How to eliminate opportunities for duplication and confusion inherent in ServiceNow's modular request architecture

Planning the portal

When planning your Request fulfillment portal it is easy to get caught up in discussions about first mapping all your business services, integrating with Assets management and Procurement, etc.

But unless you already have those processes in place and in a system trying to do all those things in tandem with your request portal project in ServiceNow could spell disaster, or unnecessarily postpone your go-live.

At Al Jazeera we went live with Incident management and worked to go live with Request fulfillment within weeks afterwards, considering it to be the true glory. But it did not work that way and seeing how big a challenge it actually was to stabilize Incident management in ServiceNow it was decided to focus on on-boarding all critical teams in the department first and making sure they were accustomed to managing incidents in ServiceNow with the service desk as the Single Point of Contact (SPOC) for all IT requests, including ERP's. Then only came Request fulfillment, more than a year later.

Lesson learned, when we finally launched the portal at Al Jazeera we resisted the temptation to integrate it with Assets management. In fact as of 2017, the two are still not fully integrated even though both processes are managed in ServiceNow.

Other ServiceNow customers also shared similar experiences. At the University in California for example, IT had launched ServiceNow with Request fulfillment, Knowledge, and Incident management all at once but then within weeks they had to disable service requests in ServiceNow, citing spam and customer dissatisfaction, abandoned Knowledge, and focused on just using plain simple Incident tickets both to record incidents and requests[2] (as we also did at Al Jazeera).

Also at CERN "It was decided to simplify the Request fulfillment process in order to achieve easier acceptance by the CERN user community." [3]

If those stories offer any insight as you approach your Request fulfillment project, remember that you are not in a marathon to implement ITIL basic processes and that a period of adjustment, customization, and improvement will normally follow the launch. Once things stabilize, build on.

User journey

In order to understand all the key elements of Request fulfillment in ServiceNow here are the steps of a typical request in ServiceNow. After this overview each element will be discussed separately.

1. Requester goes to the request **portal** through which she can request stuff.

2. She navigates to the **form** for the item or service that she wants, fills it and submits her request. She could also add the item to the shopping cart, request more items, and finally check out.

3. A **Request** record is created in ServiceNow for her request and goes through the **Request workflow**.

4. The request workflow will automatically trigger an **Approval request** to the line manager of the requester if her request crosses a certain price threshold.

---

[2]https://community.servicenow.com/docs/DOC-1338
[3]Z. Toteva et al., "Service management at CERN with Service-Now,"

5. Once the manager approves the Request, the **Requested item workflow** will be triggered for the **Requested item** (RITM). If more than one item was requested, a workflow for each requested item will be triggered at the same time.

6. If the RITM requires special approval, an **Approval request** will be triggered for it.

7. Once in the fulfillment phase of the order, the RITM workflow will create one or more **Catalog tasks** to procure and deliver the Requested item to the requester.

8. Once all Requested items have been delivered, the Request is closed.

As shown above, to request and fulfill a request, your customers, management, and your resolver teams will be subjected to multiple ServiceNow interfaces and records. To control all this, there is one workflow that defines the flow of all Requests (REQ) as well as workflows that define the approval and fulfillment process for each Requested item (RITM).

Each completed Request (REQ) in ServiceNow will have left behind all of the following records:

- Request record (REQ)

- Requested items records (RITMs)

- Approval requests for REQ and for RITMs

- Catalog tasks

Since things are already complex it is important that you strive to simplify things at each step as discussed below.

Front-end examples

The Request catalog is the portal to which you point your end users to make their requests. It is where they choose the item they want, fill the form for it, and submit their request.

It needs to be easy to navigate so that users can successfully identify the service they need, fill the respective form, and submit the request. Otherwise even if they intended to follow your process and submit their request via the portal, they may not be able to do it.

When reaching out to the service desk it is not always clear to the requester if they are reporting an issue about something that should have been but is not, or if they are requesting something new. For example, an employee may need to make international phone calls but when she finds out that she cannot do them from her phone extension, she may report it as an issue. However, from a service desk perspective, this may be considered a request and will require management approval (and cost center accounting). For this, as shown in the examples below, front-end portals often blend the ability to request new services with the ability to report new issues.

There is a lot of variety in structure, layout, and content of Request portals from organization to organization or even from one business unit to another. Within the Volkswagen group, Audi's portal is different from that of Porsche's, yet different from that of other brands in the group.

Depending on the size of your organization and your users' expectations, your Requests portal may be considered the *face of IT* (or the entire organiza-tion), and it may thus need to be customized, or be embedded into an existing intranet portal that your users already access. If that is the case, you can build your Request fulfillment portal directly in your existing intranet portal and just send the requests to ServiceNow for processing.

Al Jazeera's portal

At Al Jazeera, the service desk portal (see Figures 6-1 and 6-2) is accessible from the corporate intranet for staff members to preview the available ser-vices and request them by filling out the dedicated forms. The portal also provides one-click access for reporting issues.

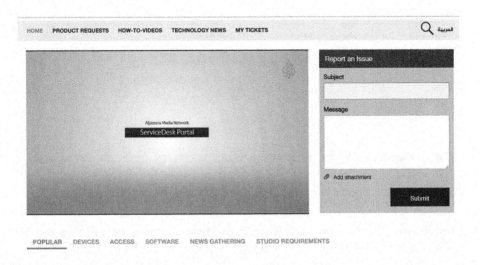

Figure 6-1. Request portal at Al Jazeera is available in English and Arabic.

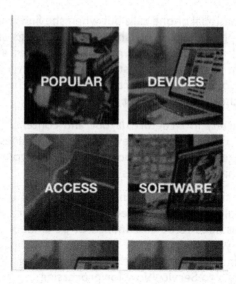

Figure 6-2. Request Portal at Al Jazeera built into the SharePoint intranet is responsive.

CERN Service Portal

The CERN Service Portal (Figure 6-3) offers access to all services offered by the research organization, lists the contact details of the service desk, and offers a search box as the primary interface. After all, CERN is all about finding answers to the secrets of the universe!

Figure 6-3. CERN Service Portal. `https://cern.service-now.com/service-portal/`

Some forms on the portal are Record producers, that is, based on a set of questions in the form, either an Incident or a Request will be logged.

Harvard University IT services

The IT services portal at Harvard University (Figure 6-4) combines access to information about the offered services together with links to requesting those services.

Figure 6-4. Harvard Univerity IT (HUIT) Services Portal. huit.harvard.edu/services

UC Davis portal

Like the portal at Harvard, the UC Davis portal (Figure 6-5) integrates the knowledge base with the requests catalog. First and foremost, it is a one-stop front-end to all IT services offered, even though many of the listed Services do not lead to a fillable ServiceNow form, but instead to a page that provides information about the service and instructions on how to request it (for example emailing software@ucdavis.edu). Other links on the portal can take you directly to external service providers such as Office365.

Figure 6-5. IT Service Catalog for the University of California Davis. `http://itcatalog.ucdavis.edu/`

Volkswagen iServe

At the Volkswagen Group, each car brand has its own portal (see examples in Figures 6-6 and 6-7). Like at Al Jazeera emphasis is on quick access to the request forms of the desired service or item.

Figure 6-6. Audi Serviceshop for requesting IT and non-IT services.

Figure 6-7. iServe Requests portal for Volkswagen.

For internal workflows that involve a limited number of users or approvers, or where requesters themselves have work to handle in ServiceNow you may not need a glossy request portal and could more simply go with the built-in service catalog interface (see Figure 6-8). This will be the quickest to build, expand, and maintain.

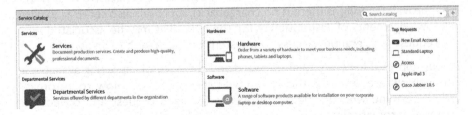

Figure 6-8. Default Service catalog accessible from within ServiceNow

Integration options

You may as well consider using your own organization's front-end portal solution and just integrate it with ServiceNow's back end.

The portal could be built using ServiceNow's CMS or Service Portal solutions, but note that unlike the option to build the catalog in ServiceNow directly, building a front end entails additional work distinct from that on the Catalog back end in ServiceNow. So you may as well consider using your own organization's front-end portal solution, such as SharePoint or Drupal and integrate it with ServiceNow's back end as some of the examples above have done.

This has the advantage that the front-end portal will be built and maintained by a team already dedicated to building front-end portals at your organization, while your ServiceNow developers can focus on the Catalog back end in ServiceNow, building workflows. If you go down this route consider these integration options:

1. Build and manage the forms in ServiceNow and have them embedded (with "iframes") in the external front-end portal page.

   This is an agile and hybrid solution that lets your ServiceNow developers control and update forms from ServiceNow without the responsibility for building the entire front-end portal. The downside is that forms may not be responsive from mobile phones.

2. Build all forms in the external portal (e.g., SharePoint) and have it send the submitted requests to ServiceNow either via Web Services or email.

Handling approvals

Even though managers in other departments tend to be concessive with granting approvals (so long as there is no chargeback), approvals also serve as explicit acknowledgements of responsibility for the risks that may be associated with the request (e.g., granting access to a system or the stealth of an asset).

If your approval logic is straightforward and the lines of reporting available in ServiceNow are accurate, then you could rely on ServiceNow to automatically determine who the right approver is for each request and collect the approval automatically.

However if you are in a situation where determining who should approve a particular request is somewhat complicated because, for example, actual reporting lines may differ from those declared in the HR systems, or because too many factors would need to be considered (e.g., approval required depends also on the seniority of the requester) then automating the approval logic in ServiceNow may not work for you. Consider this flexible approach instead:

1. The request form explains the type of approval required (e.g., Department manager) and asks the requester to name her approver (see Figure 6-9).

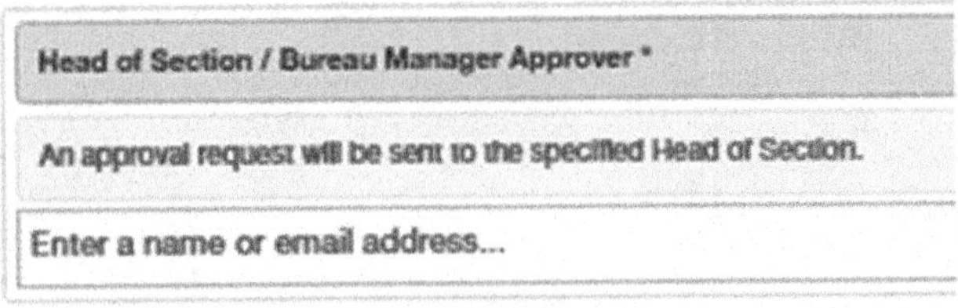

Head of Section / Bureau Manager Approver *

An approval request will be sent to the specified Head of Section.

Enter a name or email address...

Figure 6-9. Field in a catalog form requesting the approver to specify who her Head of section is

2. An approval request is automatically sent to the suggested approver.

3. The service desk verifies if the named approver is the right one and if not informs the requester.

4. The request is approved once the service desk verifies that the correct approver has been named, and the approval is obtained.

This approach is efficient in that approval requests are sent automatically as soon as the request is submitted, on the fair expectation that the requester knows who her boss is (department manager, bureau manager or whichever approval level is requested).

As such, you eliminate the chance for delays caused by ServiceNow incorrectly sending the approval request to the wrong person (e.g., a manager on leave and no delegate set in ServiceNow).

The need for the service desk to review the suggested approver may be protested as a bottleneck. But note how neither the service desk needs to wait for the suggested approver to respond, nor does the approver need to wait for the service desk verification to approve. The two can happen simultaneously (see Figure 6-10).

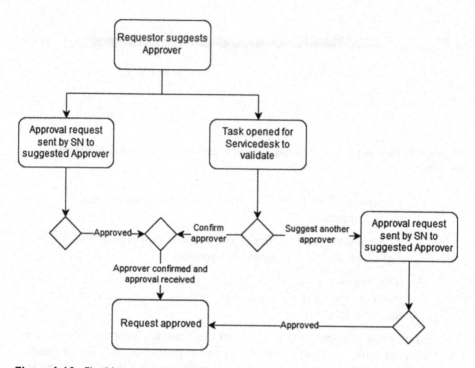

Figure 6-10. Flexible approval workflow if you do not have perfect information in ServiceNow

Duplicate approvals

ServiceNow may collect multiple approvals possibly from the same manager for the same request:

1. If the request crosses a certain expense threshold, then an approval request can be sent to obtain approval for the budget expenditure (Figure 6-11).

TO APPROVE OR REJECT THE REQUEST
To send your approval click on one of the following links and it will open a new email window; Type your comments and click on SEND.

APPROVE REQ0030568

REJECT REQ0030568

Figure 6-11. Approval Requests in ServiceNow can be comfortably approved or rejected directly by email

2. If the Requested item (RITM), for example access to a particular system or shared folder requires approval from the line manager of the requester, or the system owner, then another approval request will be triggered for the Requested item.

To avoid the annoying and inefficient duplication of approval requests, you may customize ServiceNow to skip the second approval if it is going to be sent to the same person that just approved the request. But then you lose the flexibility of approving single RITMs and rejecting others; it's a trade-off.

Bypass or modify approval

Especially when you first pilot and introduce your portal, your service desk may have to fill in request forms on behalf of requesters on the phone, or when the request is received by the service desk already with the necessary approvals.

On such occasions, even if your service desk logs the request on behalf of the requester, ServiceNow would, by default, trigger and wait on the approver to approve the request. To avoid this, you can provide the service desk with the option to bypass approval and move straight into fulfillment.

This could be done with a checkbox on forms that is visible only to service desk analysts which, once checked, would bypass approval and move straight-away to fulfillment. Alternatively, they could set the Requested by and the Approver fields to be the same so that no approval request is sent.

Detailed approval requests

In the email notification that is sent to the requester upon logging a request it would be useful to include a copy of the form(s) that were filled in. It makes the email much more valuable for reference, in case of disputes or issues, and for sharing.

The same goes for approval requests; laying out the entire request directly in the email sent to the approver will make it easier to approve and review the request (see figure 6-12).

Approval Request

Dear Mohamed,

Gabriele Kahlout request of below requires your review and approval:

Laptop for Gabriele Kahlout - REQ0037948

Requested Item :
Laptop

Do you already have a computer ?
Yes, I have a laptop

Laptop Type ?	Temporary Or Permanent :
Windows	Permanent

Figure 6-12. Filled form is sent in the approval request email

Collaborating on requests

As outlined above, for each request there will be a Request record as well as at least one Requested item record. Then there will also be Catalog tasks for the fulfillment and delivery of the requests.

Each of those ticket types can be assigned and has comments, work notes, and email notifications. When an analyst on the fulfillment side wants to update the requester, on which comments fields should she type? How can she put the request on hold?

In the cited examples where IT had to backtrack on its request portal, one key issue that upset customers with requests was the level of "spam" they received from ServiceNow.

To avoid confusion and duplication, I recommend simplifying and consolidating the channels of communication for requests as follows:

1. **Use Catalog tasks to assign work on Requests.**

    Request and Requested item records are not actionable records; they may be pending approval or may have work in progress as tracked in a Catalog Task generated by the workflow. The assignable unit of work for a request is the Catalog task.

    It will be confusing if Requests are assigned; assign only Catalog tasks. If there is a need to assign new work about a Request, a new Catalog task under the Request can be created and assigned.

2. **Unify on only one user-communication channel per request.**

   Potentially, each Request, Requested item, Approval request, and even Catalog task can have its own communication thread and watch list members, and so messages and replies could easily be fragmented across all those tickets. A simpler solution is to maintain that all user communication with the requester gets posted to the Request's comments thread and only the Request record (REQ) generates the email notifications that are sent to the requester.

   Anything that gets posted as a reply to an Approval request or to a Requested item should be posted as a Request comment (see Figure 6-13).

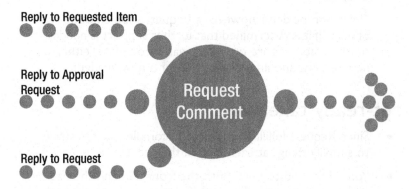

Figure 6-13. All communication with the user is consolidated in the Request ticket

3. **Show requesters only one number for their Request**

   Have all customer-facing notifications sent about a request carry the REQ number, not the RITM. The notification may be triggered based on activity in the Requested item (RITM) workflow, but you only show the end user the Request number.

4. **Task to attend unexpected requester comments**

   Finally, consider what happens if the requester writes a comment on the Request while it is pending approval, and there is no Catalog task open for it yet.

Because the Request is not assigned to anyone the update will go unnoticed. In such a scenario you could:

1. Assign the request to the service desk to handle the requester comments. The problem is that once the service desk replies what should it do with the Request ticket in its queue?

2. Open a Catalog task for the service desk to review and handle the requester's inquiry. If new inquiries come in for the same request, re-open the same Task.

5. **Replies to closed requests**

Once a Request is complete email replies to it can be handled the same way as email replies to closed incidents, showing up in the Feedback list for the service desk (see Chapter 4).

Unlike for incidents however, a Request should not be re-opened. If it is determined that further support is needed, or that the support provided was incomplete, either a new request should be submitted or a new incident.

Tweet-ready takeaways

- Since Request fulfillment is already complex as it is, strive to simplify things at each step of the process.

- You don't have to build both the front end and the back end of your portal in ServiceNow; you can integrate with your intranet portal.

- Even if your approval logic cannot be automated in ServiceNow, you can have a flexible and semi-automatic approval process in ServiceNow.

- Keep it simple and unify on only one user-communication channel per request.

- Expect to receive unexpected messages!

Reporting

How to make the most of your ServiceNow data without being cheated

The best way to change long-term behavior is with short-term feedback.

—Seth Godin[1]

If you are migrating to ServiceNow from another ITSM tool your transition plan may include the re-creation in ServiceNow of the most useful reports that you relied on in the previous tool to measure performance and prioritize resources.

In this chapter I advocate that you seize this opportunity to liberate reports from being a management thing only and ensure that individual contributors and team leads can make the most out of the data captured in ServiceNow in their daily operations.

At the management level, this is also an opportunity to open up and standardize the reports used, ensuring consistent calculation methods are used and best practices are shared.

What is particularly exciting about reporting from actual data is that it will often uncover the all too wide gap between what people say they do, need, or prefer and what their actual behavior indicates.

---

[1]http://sethgodin.typepad.com/seths_blog/2014/08/short-term-long-term.html

© Gabriele Kahlout 2017

G. Kahlout, *Spinning Up ServiceNow*, DOI 10.1007/978-1-4842-2571-4_7

In previous chapters I talked about the unfortunate fate of many ITSM tools and improvement initiatives that end up with eventual abandonment. You can track in ServiceNow the breadth and depth of users' adoption and use this insight to take action before it's too late.

The same metrics can also be used repeatedly each time you introduce a new process (and ticket type in ServiceNow) to report on process compliance in the early stages of adoption and gear action accordingly.

Reports cannot be trusted blindly however; data can be skewed to show management what they want without delivering a real improvement. You will see examples of how misleading data can be and discuss what you can do about it.

In this chapter:

1. Actionable threshold monitors: Reports are not only for management; with live performance indicators on the home page of your team they can take action at the right time before the data becomes a negative statistic on management dashboards.

2. ITSM 'Guinness' records: Individual contributors may be less interested in overall trends but they generally can be motivated to catch up and top their proximal peers in setting the record for best of their peers.

3. User adoption trends: Understand how wide your users' adoption of ServiceNow really is and how deep.

4. True customer satisfaction: Customer satisfaction surveys are bogus; you can however know more about process effectiveness from the data.

Actionable threshold monitors

Knowing how many SLAs your team breached last week is good but letting your team know how many SLAs are about to breach in the next two hours and acting upon that is even better.

People in live operations normally tend to have a low interest in reporting and often consider it the domain of management. But in reality they, not management, are the ones in front of customers and they have a direct opportunity for driving positive results, given appropriate motivation and direction. Putting this into practice in ServiceNow you can:

1. Create a filtered report that focuses on a particular threshold that you target (e.g., number of SLAs breaching within two hours);

2. Synthesize the report into a compact widget and pin it on the ServiceNow home page of your team;

3. Keep an eye on the live widget and based on the reading on the widget prioritize their next action. You can also put this on a headsup display on the wall with auto-refresh so more people can see them.

This way, rather than just pick their next action from a queue of undifferentiated tickets, or from the colleague who keeps stopping by the desk asking for favors they can take appropriate action based on the reading in the widget.

The Speedometer below for example is an out-of-box report that indicates how many open P1 tickets there are currently. Clicking on the number in the report will list those P1 tickets for drilling down into actionable details. The widget could be on the service desk home page so that analysts can actively follow up with all teams that have P1 open tickets and possibly chip in to keep the customer informed while resolvers are intently focused on fixing the issue (see Figures 7-1 and 7-2).

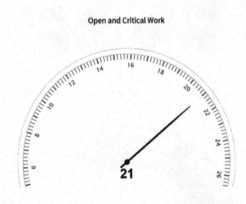

Figure 7-1. Out-of-box speedometer showing number of open P1 tickets

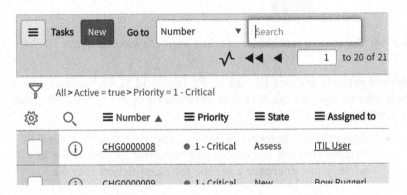

Figure 7-2. List of filtered tickets shown once you click on the speedometer shown in Figure 7-1

Other teams also would benefit from filtered reports on their home page but filtered to show only their team's tickets. For example Figure 7-3 shows how many open tickets the team has assigned that have breached SLA, or breaching within the next 10 hours. Grouped by assignee it should compel the individual contributor to clear his queue quickly.

Alternatively the dial in Figure 7-4 provides a much simpler indication of open tickets with SLAs breached or about to breach.

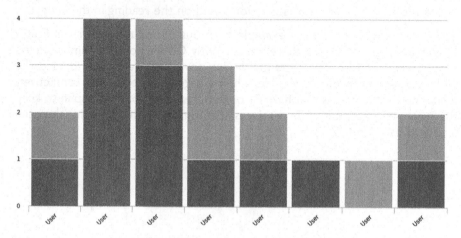

Figure 7-3. Live monitors of open tickets with breached or breaching soon SLAs

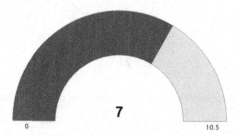

Figure 7-4. Dial showing total number of tickets with SLAs about to breach

Threshold reports are not limited to P1 fires and SLAs. You can create live reports also to keep an eye on other absolute or relative thresholds that you do not want to exceed:

- Aging tickets: Before you get an escalation about a ticket that fell through the cracks and remained neglected for a while, you can create a sensor for open tickets that have

not been updated in more than a month (or week), and
when you see one take action.

- Contracts expiring soon (see Figure 7-5): If you manage
  your contracts in ServiceNow, you can keep group contracts by how soon they will be expiring, and take appropriate renewal or switch action.

- Actual ServiceNow user experience:Are users experienc-
  ing slowness in ServiceNow? Poor instance performance
  can become a serious issue as more people depend on
  ServiceNow.You can keep an eye on actual users' experience of slowness in ServiceNow as shown below in
  figures 7-6 and 7-7, and further discussed in Appendix B.
  With live widgets such as those the ServiceNow administrator (or service desk) can gauge if ServiceNow is
  currently much slower than usual (so escalate) or if it's
  just a singular issue.

- ServiceNow fulfillment users count: As discussed in
  Chapter 3, you can pin to your home page a widget that
  tracks the number of active users in ServiceNow.

Figure 7-5. Home page shortcuts to contract that are expiring soon

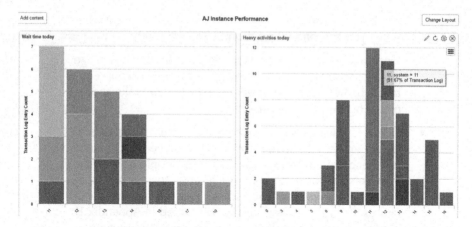

Figure 7-6. On a troubling day you can preview in which hours slowness was most experienced and compare if it coincided with long-running system transactions

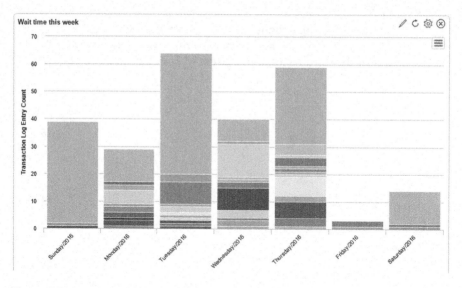

Figure 7-7. Bar chart showing how many times users had to wait every day of the week

ITSM records

Still on the topic of useful reporting for those actually on the job, you can harness data not only to guide the team to tame SLA and P1 fires as they emerge; you can use reports to motivate individual contributors to act in plausible ways out of their own initiative.

Studies show that showing people how they compare to their proximal peers (such as their neighbors or colleagues at work) on a particular metric or on a desired behavior is a powerful way to influence their behavior. Seeing what similar others are doing gives people the motivation to do that little bit more that will put them in line with their peers.

For example, in a study on 290 households in San Marcos, California, researchers informed the households about their energy consumption and offered practical tips on how to conserve energy. Some households were also told that their energy consumption was higher than that of their neighbors on average.[2]

When researchers went back to check the energy consumption readings for the neighborhood they found that the households that were told that they were consuming above average had noticeably reduced their energy consumption. Knowing that they were consuming more than their neighbors directly influenced their behavior for the better.

Back to ITSM, you can influence individual contributors to log and assign tickets to themselves by showing them that others in the department are doing it.

If you want service desk analysts to handle more tickets by themselves and escalate fewer tickets to higher tiers, show them a statistic about how some analysts do that successfully more than they do.

In ServiceNow, you can create live reports that compare individual contributors or teams to each other and make sure those lagging behind in the desired metrics are shown the way for catch up. For example, you can regularly communicate who in the team (or department) has had:

- highest number of tickets assigned;
- highest number of tickets closed;
- highest participation in tickets;
- highest number of change requests;
- highest number of tickets resolved on the spot (FCR).

Because numbers could be low in a particular day or week it may be more encouraging to compare performance to all-time records in the department, or the all-time running total, like in the *Guinness World Records*.

You may think of such motivational tactics for kids not worthy of management attention. They actually work in serious contexts also and lead to the positive change that management seeks.

---

[2]http://journals.sagepub.com/doi/pdf/10.1111/j.1467-9280.2007.01917.x

In the California study cited above, all households were told what the average energy consumption was in the neighborhood was but the group for which significant positive change was tracked they had also added a smiley face (☺) subtly indicating that being below their peers average was ☹.

At Al Jazeera, the Service Management team deployed the motivational tactics and ServiceNow reports mentioned above. For some time, the engineer logging the most change requests was even prized with chocolates while comparison reports between teams were shown regularly in CAB meetings.

In further testimony on how peer reports influence people, some analysts also reached out to me privately to understand how they were doing relative to their peers.

Metrics from the reports are also taken in consideration in the quarterly and yearly review of individuals' performance.

Measuring user adoption

You are reading this book because your challenge is to get people to use ServiceNow. Here are metrics you can use to track progress towards your goal.

1. How many people have been assigned tickets?

The number of people with assigned tickets indicates the breadth of adoption across your fulfiller teams. You may have assigned ITIL licenses to all your IT department, but how many of them actually have had a ticket assigned? You may be surprised.

To get a ticket assigned in ServiceNow is to work on ServiceNow. Over time, the number of people that had at least one (or ten) tickets assigned in the past week has to approach the number of working people in your department. If it is not, it means people are not really using it.

Another indicator about the breadth of usage is how many people have logged in to ServiceNow. Again, you may be surprised to note how infrequently some people log in to ServiceNow.

2. How many tickets per assignee a week

The first metric was to determine the breadth of ServiceNow adoption amongst your ServiceNow team and identify those who in reality have not got any work done on the tool.

The next natural dimension is to measure the depth of usage: those that have got a ticket assigned in ServiceNow, how many tickets they have assigned per week?

You can use this metric each time you introduce a new process. For example, you first ask how many Incident tickets people have assigned. Once you introduce Change management, then you ask how many Change requests has each engineer logged?

For example, you may easily discover that six months since you launched your Change management policy, people barely log 1.5 changes a month on average. When you see this, you know it's not working.

How many self-service users?

The strategy preached in Chapter 4 for automatically creating incidents via email eliminates the need for callers to use ServiceNow. So for Incident management, your self-service adoption challenge is sorted from the beginning. That's not the case for Request fulfillment however.

There, end users need to go to the self-service portal and submit their service requests from there.

To measure the effectiveness of your Request portal, you can track in ServiceNow the number of request tickets that have been logged by the requester (requested for = opened by) as in Figure 7-8 below.

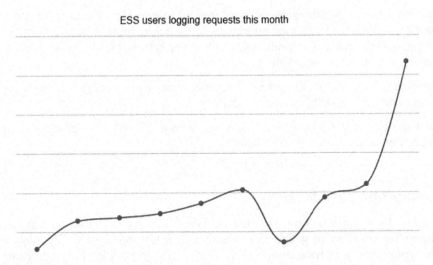

Figure 7-8. Spline trend report showing the number of requests opened in 2016 through Al Jazeera's self-service portal by non-IT staff

Tracking those metrics will be particularly important in the initial ground-breaking weeks and months of the initiative. If you see that about the same number of tickets has been logged this month as in previous months and you know that a lot more work is actually going around the organization then you know you have a user adoption problem.

In such a case you may decide to intensify training, reconsider a decision made about not automatically rerouting all email tickets sent to ServiceNow (Chapter 4), reduce the complexity involved in updating tickets in ServiceNow, backtrack on the number of processes launched at once, etc.

Once you get through this initial phase you can use the same metrics again, but to track compliance to the specific process that you have just introduced (e.g., Change management).

Management reports

From reports management want to see that month-to-month, quarter-to-quarter, or year-to-year things are improving. They want to see that things are getting better than they used to be and not staying constant (or worsening). This is what trend reports are for.

> "The key drivers of future revenue growth are trending positive, and we remain confident in Twitter's future."
>
> —Jack Dorsey, founder and CEO of Twitter

Generally speaking, management is interested in two things: customer satisfaction going up and costs of operation going down (operational efficiency). Of course the two are at odds with each other, but that's why they invest in process automation and training.

Trend reports could also be used to identify time-specific correlations to use in rota and maintenance windows planning.

For example do you know which is typically your busiest hour of the day? Is December a busier month than April?

Customer satisfaction

Besides the traditional how-satisfied-were-you surveys, you can look at the data in ServiceNow to gauge how satisfied or frustrated customers may be with your service as have done the California researchers in the study going back and checking the actual energy consumption readings

From an Incident management perspective the most important thing for the customer is to have her issue solved as quickly as possible (all other things being equal, e.g., politeness). Even if you consider Request fulfillment, there too the speed by which you deliver their request is a key target.

Based on ITIL recommendations, ServiceNow provides reports on the following Key Performance Indicators (KPIs) to measure customer satisfaction:

1. *Average incident resolution time:* Measures how quickly incidents are resolved on average

2. *First time resolution rate:* Measures how many incidents are solved on the spot, for example during the customer's first call

3. *Incident resolution within SLA:* You told stakeholders that you resolve most issues within X hours. Are you keeping that promise?

4. *Number of repeated incidents:* Do you fix issues permanently or do they keep happening again shortly after you say they have been fixed.

5. *Involvement required:* I also propose a more applicable variant of FTR which measures how much user involvement it takes to resolve an incident even if it was not solved on the spot. That is how many times on average did the caller have to leave a comment to the ticket before the issue is solved?

   This can be measured in ServiceNow with a custom metric that counts the number of comments the customer had to leave per ticket and allows you to identify those service desk analysts that keep putting the ticket on hold pending user input, instead of obtaining the requested details by themselves (which they often can).

Misleading data

In terms of issues customers would much rather have no incidents in the first place! So the most important metric would be to track the total number of incidents and make sure that on month-to-month there are fewer incidents.

Counting that in ServiceNow is very easy; the problem is that it can be misleading. Are there fewer incidents in ServiceNow because there are fewer issues in practice or is it because fewer have been logged in the system?

Jamie Duncalf, IT Operations Manager at TransAlta, exemplifies this thinking by saying "we saw an immediate increase in recorded incidents. While this may seem counterintuitive, it was exactly what we wanted. It meant that our end users were comfortable reporting incidents online rather than doing an end run around our processes."[3]

---

[3]https://www.servicenow.com/content/dam/servicenow/documents/whitepapers/cs-transalta.pdf

When I worked with business users, it struck me to note how they all simply avoided reporting issues to IT even if it was to the detriment of the business or work that they were doing. We would be doing something together and an issue would show up with the software we were using; in my mind I instinctively thought of reporting a bug or a feature request but to my surprise they didn't think about it at all.

I wondered if this was just a singular experience, but Gartner and Forrester have also observed the same and estimate that 70-80% of problems impacting end users are never reported or detected, calling this the "IT visibility gap".[4]

You may find the statistic exaggerated but note that studies observing how people make decisions on the job have also found that when faced with an issue people on the job do not tend to weigh all their available options and pick one rationally.

What they do instead is take the first plausible option that comes to mind, the one that will do. Nobel Prize winner Herbert A. Simon coined this behavior as "satisficing", a combination of satisfy and suffice.

Back to Service Management: It will generally be too early to assume that all of the reportable issues are being logged in ServiceNow and so you will normally see the number of incidents—even the number of P1 incidents—going up. You can also report on:

1. Percentage of the total

What you can report on to identify if things are improving are percentages. For example, how many incidents are resolved within SLA out of the total number of incidents logged? If the percentage is going up, and so is the number of logged incidents, then things are trending in the right direction.

Apple for apple

Password resets are notoriously quick incidents sorted on the phone. For those cases, a First time resolution close to 100% is the norm.

For issues that require physically going to the user to replace hardware for example, things will typically take much longer. But reporting on metrics calculated from the average for data skewed like this will be misleading.

You will get a meaningful report if you examine singular ticket categories separately so you are comparing apples for apples.

You may for example categorize password resets separately, take aim at reducing password reset incidents by introducing a self-service password reset solution and then again use reports to measure the impact of the solution.

---

[4]http://www.aternity.com/aternity-central/business-transformation-starts-frictionless-user-experience/

Conflicting interests

Some reports will be based on what *close code* the analyst used to close the ticket (see figure 7-9). This makes your report only as accurate as the people logging the ticket.

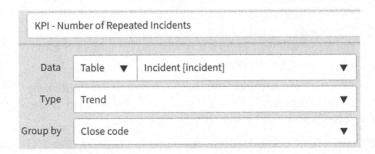

Figure 7-9. ServiceNow's out-of-box report on repeated incidents is based on the close code used by the analyst to close the ticket. So the report will only be as good as the input. An alternative that may uncover repeat incidents is to check on the number of incidents logged per caller and assigned to the same assignment group. If a caller had many tickets assigned to the same group in a short span of time, it may well be a repeat incident.

Measuring repeat incidents for example can be tricky because the issue may present itself in a slightly different context each time. But the team logging the ticket may not log it as a repeat incident and if asked, argue that the two issues may be similar but are technically different.

It is also not in their interest to log repeat incidents. Why didn't they fix it the first time?

The ideal solution to those conflict-of-interest dilemmas is to have another party not invested in the matter log the repeat incident. In practice however this may not be worthwhile.

So it is important that you watch out for reports that are based on human input and take them with a grain of salt, or exclude them completely from your reporting suite.

Operational efficiency

If the average time it takes your team to resolve incidents is falling then things must be operating more smoothly under the hood.

Often times however, the average may not be falling and you need a more detailed analysis to understand why it takes your team so long to resolve incidents (or deliver on requests). Enter the domain of operation efficiency reports.

Factors that delay an incident resolution may be organization-specific but two essential ones are covered by ServiceNow Out-of-box reports:

1. *Incidents assigned more than once:* This report indicates how long it takes to identify the team responsible to fix the issue. Ideally, an incident should be directly assigned to the team responsible for solving it from the beginning. Otherwise the longer the ticket stays in limbo, the longer the issue will wait before it is worked on and so the longer it will take to solve.

2. *Remotely resolved incidents:* Issues that require mobilizing on-site support will take longer to resolve than issues solved remotely by the service desk.

The auto-assignment configurations discussed in chapters 4 and 11 take aim at reducing re-assignments by automatically identifying the correct assignment group for an incident. You could track the effectiveness of those automations using the above reports.

Furthermore, from those reports you may observe that a large number of similar tickets get regularly escalated from the service desk but that given adequate tools and access could be solved by the desk directly. For example granting access to modify user details in Active Directory or in ServiceNow (see Chapter 3).

Standard dynamic reports

If you ask team leaders about their reporting needs, you will definitely come to this conclusion: most of their reporting needs are the same.

They all want to know how many SLAs their team has breached, how many tickets the team processed, who handled most of the tickets, which tickets kept being re-opened from the caller, what tickets are outstanding for a long time, etc.

When reports are created based on the requirements from teams, demand that instead of creating reports custom-built for teams, only create dynamic reports that display different data based on the person logged in to view the report (see figure 7-10).

Figure 7-10. Dynamic filters allow the report to show different data based on who is viewing the report

Dynamic reports allow you to ensure the same reports and calculations are used by all teams across the department or organization, and that you can immediately on-board new teams in ServiceNow without having to create duplicate reports for them. You can also share new useful reports requested by one team with other teams.

Also, if your department has identified a number of key metrics that it wants to improve in dynamic reports will allow teams in the department and even individual contributors to measure their progress against the same metrics and using the same calculation methods.

If you examine some out-of-box reports you will notice that some include javascript:getMyGroups() in a filter that expects a group, for example the Assignment group as shown in Figure 7-11.

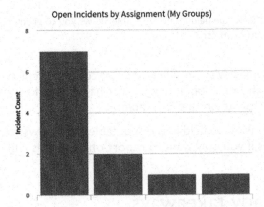

Figure 7-11. *Open Incidents by Assignment (My Groups)* report shows the tickets assigned to the teams the logged-in user viewing the report belongs to

This string allows the report to be dynamically populated with the groups the person logged in to view the report is a member of.

In Chapter 3 we also discussed the concept of setting a primary group for each user. Use this string to create dynamic reports that only show the tickets of one's primary group:

```
javascript:gs.getUser().getRecord().getValue('u_primary_group')
```

Every ITIL user can create a report in ServiceNow while users with a report-group role can create and share reports with others.

Report-admins and report-global can also create reports visible to everyone such as the set of dynamic reports discussed above.

Report on all tickets

When you create a report in ServiceNow, the first thing that you have to set is on which record table you want to run the report. This can be Incident, Catalog task, Change request, User, etc.

Most of the time however, people will be interested in running reports on all tickets assigned to their team, regardless of whether they were Incidents or Catalog tasks. In this case, you will want to run your reports on the Task table (see Figure 7-12). This is because in ServiceNow every Incident is automatically a Task, and so are Problem tickets, Catalog tasks, etc.

Figure 7-12. The Task type field in the Task table allows you to group or filter tickets by type (Incident, Change, Problem, etc.)

ServiceNow comes with an *Open and Critical Work* report that runs on the Task table and shows all open tickets that have the priority set as P1. You can create similar reports on the Task table.

There is also a Task type field in the Task table that allows you to group by certain ticket types if you only want to report on Problems and Change Requests.

Tweet-ready takeaways

- Liberate reports from being a management thing only and ensure contributors can make the most out of the data in their daily operations.

- Showing people how they compare to their proximal peers on a particular metric is a powerful way to influence their behavior.

- Instead of how-satisfied-were-you surveys look at the data in ServiceNow to gauge how satisfied or frustrated customers really were.

- To get tickets assigned is to work on ServiceNow. If the number of people that had tickets assigned is low, it means people are not using it.

- The longer the ticket stays in limbo between teams, the longer the wait before it is worked on and the longer it will take to solve.

- If you ask team leaders about their reporting needs, you will definitely come to this conclusion: most of their reporting needs are the same.

After go-live

Adopting ITIL is never finished as you will always adapt your processes to new situations, the big benefit is that you do it in a controlled way, and not on an ad-hoc basis.

—Pink Elephant[1]

From the day of go-live people will report issues and suggest enhancements. Part III covers how to go about fulfilling them while maintaining a stable live environment, and how to manage developers and stakeholders.

---

[1]https://www.pinkelephant.co.za/it-service-management-2/implementing-an-itsm-tool/

Customization Process

What you will be doing on ServiceNow after go-live and how to go about it effectively

> In the end, a strategy is nothing but good intentions unless it's effectively implemented.
>
> —Clayton Christensen, Harvard professor and author on innovation[1]

ServiceNow is promoted as an extremely flexible software platform, and it is. Still as in other web applications changes made to it can immediately affect all users on the platform. For this how you go about implementing changes to your ServiceNow instance can be a deal breaker in the success of ServiceNow at your organization and in your reputation managing this enterprise application.

In my experience for example spam or irrelevant emails accidentally sent from ServiceNow could lead to high-profile escalations and cause a publicity blunder for the department and those responsible.

---

[1]Christensen, Clayton M., "How will you measure your life?" Speech to Harvard University Business School graduating class, 2010, USA

© Gabriele Kahlout 2017
G. Kahlout, Spinning Up ServiceNow, DOI 10.1007/978-1-4842-2571-4_8

On such an occasion I recall handling the apology to a high-profile TV presenter that emailed complaining about spam emails that she received from ServiceNow.

Furthermore, if the resolution of a critical issue is somehow delayed because of ServiceNow, confidence in the system will be eroded and people will be justified in bypassing it, while questions will be raised about ServiceNow's fitness for the organization (or your ability to manage it).

In this chapter:

1. Why companies customize: The philosophical and practical reasons why out-of-box is only part of what you signed up for, with real-world examples.

2. Essential process: What your stakeholders want you to tell developers.

3. Requirements: How to be like Steve Jobs and set the record straight for new customizations and how to prioritize stakeholders wish lists.

4. Deploy like a pro: The rigor you need your administrator to stick to in order to safeguard production data and users.

Customization vs. configuration

The definition of what is a customization versus what is just a configuration is widely debated by ServiceNow practitioners and the industry at large. Let me clear my thoughts on it before we move further.

Software platform vendors tend to consider most of their clients' changes as configurations of their mighty out-of-box functionality but when you contact their support helpdesk for help with something that you have changed in your instance you will often be told that your change is considered custom development and thus they cannot help you with it.

So, configurations can be defined as changes in your ServiceNow instance that are made using options built into the ServiceNow user interface for which you can normally get support from ServiceNow's HI helpdesk. When the change/configuration does not work as expected and it's reproducible, it may be filed as a platform bug in ServiceNow.

Examples of such supported-for-free configurations may include the creation of a new Access control rule, a new Workflow using the Workflow engine, layout re-arrangement of fields, or the creation of new fields.

A customization is when you modify code, or add new one. Changes to the code of inbound email actions, new Client scripts, or Business rules that have code in them are all examples of customizations. ServiceNow HI will normally shun away from debugging your code. If it involves scripting, it's a customization.

The good new is that with every new release of ServiceNow the list of configurations directly supported by the ServiceNow's user interface expands. Many of the things that required scripting in earlier versions can now be achieved with configuration. New releases also introduce new out-of-box features which you had to previously develop as customization in your instance.

But also the options for customization and development have increased. In fact in 2015 ServiceNow introduced a slew of tools to help developers better manage their code, while the Istanbul release introduces automated testing.

Why companies customize

Out-of-box functionality is great; you already paid for it and should use it as often as possible. However, most of the time organizations need to customize because of their unique circumstances.

In theory, you could force your service desk and organization to run with ServiceNow as is, but it's much easier to mold ServiceNow to run as suits your organization and circumstances than to coerce your organization to fit into a square hole.

As Randy Mott, chief information officer at General Motors, puts it: "*companies that win in their industries are the ones that figure out how to get ahead, because getting competitive advantage takes innovation, it takes creativity, and you're not going to get that from someone who's going to make everyone on the planet even.*"

When it comes to ServiceNow it may be sold to management on how much there is already OOB and how little configuration will be needed to meet most of the business needs, while technical folks will be invited to participate in hacking hijinks at conferences such as the CreatorCon.

It depends on your interest. Software developers tend to prefer customizing the system to perform as they specify. They take pride in their code and are sometimes accused of avoiding already existing solutions only because they were made by others (this is known as the "not invented here" syndrome).

Business people on the other hand are less interested in new technical challenges and tend to prefer ready-made solutions that can be contracted at a predictable expense and are guaranteed by reputable vendors. Many of them, acknowledge from experience however that off-the-shelf software alone is rarely sufficient to get their business going, and so they need to have some expertise in-house.

What are those customizations that we are talking about so much?

Here are three examples of the kind of customizations. You will also find more examples of customizations that ServiceNow customers typically make in Chapter 11, and even more documented online.

Many organizations like Harvard University, Berkeley, CERN, and Fermilab research centers have made some of their ServiceNow internal release notes publicly available.[2,3,4]

1. Workflow automation

All automatic behavior and values settings defined in ServiceNow can be categorized as workflow automation. The goal of workflow automations is to streamline the execution of known processes, guide users throughout it, and reduce manual steps and the chances of human error and forgetfulness.

Examples of such automations include automating the assignment of tickets based on criteria like the email address the issue was reported to, the location of the caller, or the product (Configuration item) the support request is for. A more detailed discussion of assignment logic is in Chapter 11.

Approval requests can be automatically sent based on whom the request is for and fulfillment tasks can be automatically generated and assigned based on a predefined workflow set for the requested item. For example, the termination of an employee's services could simultaneously trigger multiple tasks for the different teams responsible for the deactivation of the services the employee had.

For routine back-end workflows, you can define a workflow of actions and approvals that need to be taken in sequence to decommission a server for example (Figure 8-1).

---

[2]http://huit.harvard.edu/about-us/support-services/it-service-management
[3]http://servicenow.berkeley.edu/release-notes
[4]http://juomini.com/servicenow/

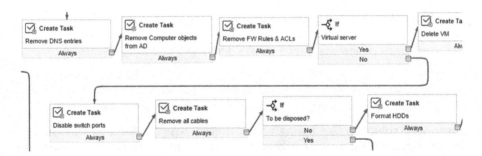

Figure 8-1. Sequence of automatically created tasks triggered by a workflow

2. Convenience and cosmetic customizations

When examined critically, many of the customizations we made at Al Jazeera were in theory unnecessary. But in practice our stakeholders found them critical for their smooth operations.

For example, prior to ServiceNow the service desk was used to receive incoming emails in a shared inbox and as the emails arrived, available agents would glance at the email and flag it to indicate that they were on it. Seeing the email flagged, other colleagues also looking at the inbox will divert their attention to other unclaimed emails (Figure 8-2).

Figure 8-2. Flags in Outlook

But when tickets started pouring in ServiceNow, there were no flags for tickets and so the agents found themselves claiming the same tickets in the queue and sometimes overwriting each others' messages and assignments.

An agent would open a ticket while another agent also had the same ticket open. Each would assign and make changes to the ticket, but would not know of other updates until after she posted her updates to the ticket.

I proposed solutions like having agents quickly assign tickets to themselves directly from the list view of tickets, or asking agents to shout the ticket they just claimed but none were deemed appropriate (Figure 8-3).

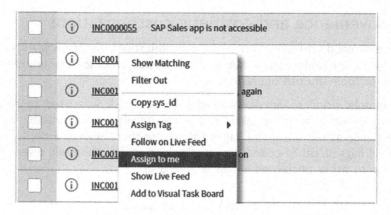

Figure 8-3. If you right-click on a ticket in a list, you can quickly assign it to yourself with one more click.

So in the end we introduced a customization that suited our service desk[5]: As soon as you open a ticket, you will be informed if someone else has also been on the ticket recently. Also, when you click to save your changes to a ticket you will be informed if someone else made new changes in the meantime, and you will be given the option to hold your changes.

In ServiceNow's newest User Interface (UI16) a similar feature has been introduced showing you who else is also viewing the ticket at the same time as you. So after upgrading to the Helsinki release our stakeholders found the new User presence functionality satisfactory, and so we removed our customization (Figure 8-4).

---

[5]The customization we introduced was based on the Simultaneous Update Alert script provided by the official ServiceNow Wiki: http://wiki.servicenow.com/index.php?title=Simultaneous_Update_Alert

Figure 8-4. The new presence feature in ServiceNow shows you how many people are currently looking at the ticket that you are also viewing

You can bet that many of the things your stakeholders want will not (yet) be in ServiceNow in a suitable fashion, and so you will have to implement them as customizations.

For another example, we also removed the impact and urgency fields from ticket forms, giving ITIL users direct control over the priority and tying each priority to an SLA. The priority itself was renamed to include the number of SLA hours associated with this priority (Figure 8-5).

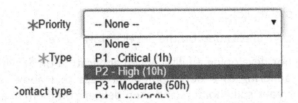

Figure 8-5. When creating a new Incident ITIL users have to manually set the priority. A P2 priority has a 10-hours SLA

We also customized the look and feel of email notifications (discussed in Chapter 5) as well as which fields show up in user and ticket preview windows.

3. Access control

Generally speaking ServiceNow may be too permissive for your teams and the kind of data dealt with. So you may introduce customizations that control who can see what (tickets confidentiality is discussed in Chapter 9).

You may also need to create new special access controls that for example give contracts administrators the capability to add new vendors in ServiceNow but not the ability to create or delete user accounts.

The examples above illustrated why making ServiceNow work to suit your organization will require configuration and sometimes also customizations. That said, think twice before allowing the development of new customizations especially if there is something similar out of the box.

Many of the configurable options in ServiceNow can have undesired side effects resulting, for example, in duplicate email notifications, as discussed in Chapters 4 and 5.

Customization process

For building "quality applications" on the ServiceNow platform, ServiceNow recommends the following development process:[6]

1. Define business requirements.

2. Define what information the application needs to track.

3. Build the application.

4. Test the application.

5. Share the application on the ServiceNow Store.

Even if you are not developing a fully-fledged application on ServiceNow, you will benefit by adhering to a development process that above all sets the expectations for your stakeholders and then delivers on them in a predicable fashion.

In essence, your stakeholders need to have clear and consistent answers to the following questions about the way customizations and changes are made to the instance:

1. How are customization requests reported and tracked?

Stakeholders can chat with you about their feature requests or bugs. But then what happens with their requests? How can they follow up on them? How do they know if and when they will be released?

An Excel spreadsheet or initial requirements document may be fine as a starting point but often there will need to be a discussion between developers, analysts, stakeholders, and testers for each new feature before the final outcome is ready. Where will you track all this?

---

[6]https://docs.servicenow.com/bundle/helsinki-application-development/
page/build/applications/reference/r_BasicDevelopmentProcess.html

2. Where will customizations be developed?

3. How do you deploy customizations?

Especially for an enterprise platform like ServiceNow on which stakeholders rely to perform their work daily, stakeholders will be anxious if you make unannounced changes on the instance while they are also using it.

As the manager of the application you want to give them the confidence that developments are made on another instance and not on the production instance, while deployments to the production instance are controlled by an open process that involves stakeholders in testing and notification.

At Al Jazeera developments are made in a non-production instance and are packaged together for deployment to the production instance at a time agreed upon by the stakeholders.

Stakeholders are also typically given a window of three days to preview and test the latest developments in the Test instance so they can report on issues they may identify before deployment to the live instance (Figure 8-6).

Figure 8-6. Customizations lifecycle

The objectives of the development process are to:

1. maximize the stability of your ServiceNow production instance through a strict development-test-release process;

2. set standards to ensure new customizations don't result in inconsistent interfaces that confuse users;

3. grant people access roles suitable for their day-to-day activities, but curb the chance of accidental mischief on your production environment;

4. in case of issues with your instance, ensure you can recover quickly;

5. maintain a non-production replica of your ServiceNow environment for development and testing;

6. avoid customizations that will make maintenance and upgrades of your ServiceNow instance difficult;

7. flexibly on-board new teams in ServiceNow without affecting present users of the system or requiring further customization.

Requirements backlog

Requirements will be coming at you from meetings with stakeholders, emails, and your own observations. It's important that you then store all of them in one place that is central and shared with your stakeholders, and that is flexible enough to keep track of related conversations and updates.

In the spirit of eating your own dog food, I recommend you track all issues and enhancement requests for your ServiceNow instance in your ServiceNow instance itself.

This is a common practice in the IT industry and it has been cited from big name companies such as Microsoft, Apple, Google, and YouTube. In 1980 the president of Apple Computers famously wrote a memo announcing:

> "Effective Immediately!! No more typewriters are to be purchased, leased etc., etc. . . . We believe the typewriter is obsolete. Let's prove it inside before we try and convince our customers."[7]

By the same token, using your own ServiceNow instance will give you and your ServiceNow developers and administrators a direct first-hand experience of managing tickets in ServiceNow both from a user perspective as well as from a resolvers' perspective. Ideally, your external partners should also use ServiceNow, as discussed in Chapter 3.

Prioritization

As with any software development project, prioritization of requirements and the management of stakeholders' expectations can be challenging.

As quoted in earlier chapters Jason Fried, co-founder of Basecamp, illustrates this common problem as follows: "*I found project-based consulting frustrating because we would work on a site for months and hand it over to the client, who would inevitably make changes and drag us through their politics. It was rare that what we actually built saw the light of day.*"[8]

---

[7]http://www.inc.com/magazine/19811001/2033.html

This is even more so in an internal organization where there is no charge for requirements and with ServiceNow, for which it is commonly perceived that everything is either already available out-of-box or can be easily accomplished through a few clicks.

Dealing With wish lists   Use time constraints to trade-off requirements

Charge and involve stakeholders in development

The software development industry has proposed many prioritization methods, including MoSCoW.

With MoSCoW, for each requirement with which you agree with the stakeholder, you also set the priority as either Must have, Should have, Could have, or Won't have.

Because most stakeholders often have too many Must-haves at Al Jazeera we instead inform stakeholders of how much effort each requirement is roughly expected to take in the upcoming development sprint so they prioritize relative to other requirements proposed for the sprint. The discussion in the backlog review would go like this:

"In two weeks, we could implement Feature X and Feature Y. Feature Z is likely to take a week on its own.

"Shall we then go ahead with X and Y for the next release, and also squeeze in a fix for J, K, and H?"

Chargeback

At Volkswagen, the director of ServiceNow told me that to prioritize requirements, he asks internal customers coming to him with new requirements and workflows to implement in ServiceNow to also bring with them the budget for the requested development.

Thanks to such an internal chargeback system, internal customers think twice before asking for complex new workflows, as well as prioritize within themselves which requirements are really going to deliver the most value to them.

---

[8]http://www.inc.com/guides/2010/11/how-to-turn-a-service-business-into-a-product-business.html

Once delivered they will already be invested to use it and make it pay off, not to look bad in front of their management for budget misuse.

Without a chargeback system, you run the risk of building features and work-flows that ultimately nobody uses, as Jason Fried said and I occasionally experienced at Al Jazeera.

If you can implement a form of internal chargeback for ServiceNow customizations, do it. If not, consider investing them as much as possible in the development and testing of their own customizations as discussed below.

The University of California, Berkeley website informs that each department using ServiceNow is responsible for the licensing fees of its staff and that as of 2017, each department will also be expected to contribute to the support and maintenance costs of ServiceNow.[9]

IKEA effect

An alternative to charging departments from their budgets is to put them in charge of the development.

Whenever possible, seek to invest requesters' own labor in achieving their requirements, such us letting them make their own changes in ServiceNow. This is after all supposed to be why Fred Luddy, ServiceNow founder, started ServiceNow in the first place:

"Ordinary people should be able to create meaningful applications for their organizations."[10]

For complex development involve them in the communication with the developers and the testing. As studies show, the more involved the stakeholder is in a fruitful project, the more they will value the outcome and the more understanding they will be of possible delays and limitations.

In a study,[11] Michael Norton et al. illustrate how irrationally people tend to value a product that they were involved in making, such as self-assembled IKEA furniture.

---

[9]https://technology.berkeley.edu/news/servicenow-funding-model

[10]http://www.businessinsider.com/servicenow-luddy-go-write-your-own-apps-2014-4

[11]Norton, Michael I.; Mochon, Daniel; Ariely, Dan (2012). "The IKEA effect: When labor leads to love" (PDF). *Journal of Consumer Psychology.* **22** (3): 453–460. doi:10.1016/j.jcps.2011.08.002.

Subjects in the study were found to be willing to pay up to 63% more for products they had assembled than for the same item assembled by others. Some participants were even found to value their own creations five times as much as another group's valuation for the same product.

That is, those who invested labor in making something, consider it much more valuable than if it were done by others.

Development and testing

Poorly designed customizations can lead to unexpected side effects in unexpected areas of the application, need rework, and offer an inconsistent user experience. In short, your ServiceNow instance can become a mess!

The responsibility for designing good solutions falls on your ServiceNow developers, but this often also requires understanding and collaboration from the client too.

As the manager of the application, you can set the expectation for both business users with requirements (yourself included) and developers for the kind of customizations you allow on the platform, and those that you reject (even if possible) in favor of simpler solutions coherent with the overall design in ServiceNow.

Role of Management   Veto complex requirements

Set standards

A wonderful example of management that understands the simplicity principle comes from a 2006 interview with Steve Jobs.

Steve Jobs was asked about Microsoft's new iPod competitor and its community-building feature. Steve Jobs dismissed it by noting how unnecessarily complicated it was:[12]

> "I've seen the demonstrations on the Internet about how you can find another person using a Zune and give them a song they can play three times. It takes forever. By the time you've gone through all that, the girl's got up and left!"

> "You're much better off to take one of your earbuds out and put it in her ear. Then you're connected with about two feet of headphone cable."

---

[12]https://signalvnoise.com/posts/52-steve-jobs-just-put-it-in-her-ear?69

The same logic reasoned by Steve Jobs can be applied to ServiceNow requirements. For example, a common issue fretted about when introducing ServiceNow to your department is which categories and sub-categories there should be.

The categories the service desk wants will undoubtedly not be the same categories the network team wants, and the same is likely to be true for each team because each team deals with different issues and has a particular world view.

In this context the please-all requirement may come as:

Show different categories based on which team the ticket is assigned to.

But this is a convoluted solution and requires twisting ServiceNow's categories by adding new tables and team-based access constraints. Why go this way?

Rather than forcing a solution on ServiceNow, it would be better to identify a solution that works with the ServiceNow default way.

A much simpler solution for example (and one that requires no coding) is to add all category options with a designated team prefix for ease of reference.

For example, categories of the service desk can be prefixed with the "SD" prefix as in "SD: Access," while Network team categories with the "NET" prefix as in "NET: Connectivity."

This way all teams have their categories, each team can easily find their categories and no convoluted ServiceNow configuration and development is required. Additionally, you could also use the category field to identify the team whose categories you want to preview in the subcategory field only.

You get the idea; encourage creative yet simple solutions to the requirements proposed by your stakeholders (Figure 8-7).

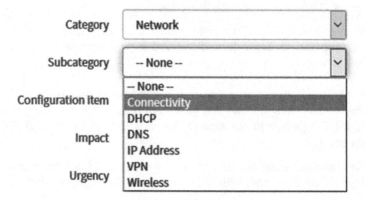

Figure 8-7. Incident subcategory used to list the Network's team categories

Other subcategories would be shown if the Category selected was Service desk (Figure 8-8).

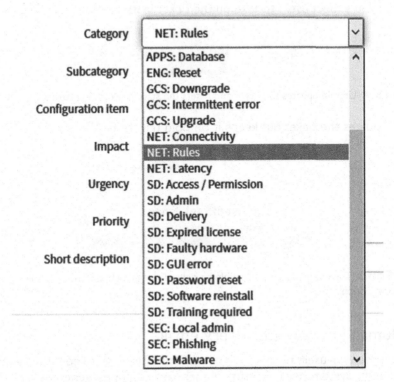

Category	NET: Rules ⌄
	APPS: Database ⌃
Subcategory	ENG: Reset
	GCS: Downgrade
Configuration item	GCS: Intermittent error
	GCS: Upgrade
	NET: Connectivity
Impact	NET: Rules
	NET: Latency
Urgency	SD: Access / Permission
	SD: Admin
Priority	SD: Delivery
	SD: Expired license
	SD: Faulty hardware
Short description	SD: GUI error
	SD: Password reset
	SD: Software reinstall
	SD: Training required
	SEC: Local admin
	SEC: Phishing
	SEC: Malware ⌄

Figure 8-8. Incident category drop-down with team-based categories prefixed with a prefix for each team for ease of identification and navigation

Consistent standards

As new feature requests come in and changes are made, your instance behavior can become unpredictable and confusing.

A principle of good application design is to minimize the thinking process your users have to go through using your application, making sure things tend to be where they expect them across the application. Applied to ServiceNow, here are some standards I recommend you adhere to when planning new changes:

1. Minimize the number of buttons on forms

As per good user interaction practice, your screen should have a very limited number of call-to-action buttons (ideally, only one).

For this, rather than add new buttons to your forms, add new options in the Context menu accessible by right-clicking the ticket header (Figure 8-10). The buttons displayed on the form should be only the most common two or three actions you expect users to take on the ticket in its current state (Figure 8-9).

Figure 8-9. Unhold updates the ticket and resets the state to Work in progress.

Hold updates the ticket but keeps it on hold (Figure 8-10).

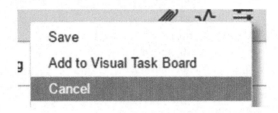

Figure 8-10. The context menu accessible by right-clicking a ticket header provides additional options.

2. Human message with every email

It's common for users to overlook email notifications received from a website or ticketing system, because many of them are computer-generated.

It is better if you set the standard for ServiceNow notifications to be only triggered with a message typed in by somebody. Once users notice that, they will be more likely to take your emails seriously and you eliminate the risk of ServiceNow inadvertently spamming your organization with computer-generated emails.

To ensure this, you would mandate that closing a ticket or putting it on hold would require the person changing the ticket status to also write a human-readable comment to the caller. Such requirements will trigger them to think more carefully about the change.

3. Limit team-specific customizations

As illustrated with categories, it is very likely that every team using ServiceNow will delight in giving you custom changes specific to their team.

They will want different notifications to be sent, different names for fields on the form, and even a different layout for the same fields.

As of the Istanbul release, ServiceNow is not built for having a different incident form for each team; it can be done creating team-specific access roles and rules, new tables or new views.

But it can grow messy and become difficult to manage. If you can, it would be better to limit team-specific customizations and ensure the layout and behavior of ticket forms shared by multiple teams be consistent for all users.

4. Transparent behavior

What happens If I write a comment? Who will be notified? Will an email be sent if I close the ticket without writing a comment? Once I submit a request, to whom will the approval request be sent?

[13] Here is an illustrative example of the sort of questions and confusion that non-transparent behavior raises in the mind of its users. As published by Harvard University IT on its website, a user asked:

> I have a question about "watcher" notifications in ServiceNow. Someone else added me (and a few others) as a watcher to this ticket INC00882705 and made work note updates four times since May. We only today received a notification email that the work notes had been updated-she closed the ticket and stated we hadn't gotten back to her. Can you explain when watcher notification emails are and aren't sent out for a ticket? In this case, the person who was updating the work notes thought that we were getting notified but in fact we were not and so the ticket went unnoticed.
>
> I've asked the user to assign tickets to our queue instead of adding us as watchers, but it would be nice to know when watcher notifications will/ won't be sent out.

Users of your system will be wondering about these questions as they use ServiceNow and it is not the feature of a good system if users feel puzzled or out of control.

For this, when you make new backed-end customizations remember to also to show information messages in context that make obvious the new unexpected behavior of the customization (Figure 8-11).

---

[13]http://huit.harvard.edu/files/huit/files/feature_report_for_snow_release_-_101614.pdf

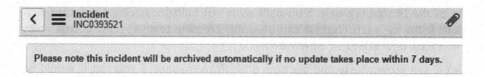

Figure 8-11. When viewing a ticket that is on hold, an information banner informs that the ticket will be automatically closed if not updated within a set number of days.

Also, whenever possible try to make things visible directly in front of the user. For example, if approval will be collected from her line manager, make that obvious in the request form and copy her in the CC of the approval request so that she can chase her manager to approve.

Development instance

ServiceNow is a flexible application and many things in it can be configured without coding. But whether coding or not, not all changes are equal.

A change to inbound email actions or the addition of one email notification may sabotage your instance processing of incoming support emails, or spam them with unexpected email notifications. A few events in which customer emails were missed are sufficient to erode trust in the application and lead to escalation to senior management.

For this, it's important to guard your production instance from uncontrolled changes to functionality shared by many users. It's better to make changes and test them in a non-production instance first, and then deploy them to the production instance in a controlled fashion.

Your license contract with ServiceNow normally provides you with two ServiceNow instances: one production instance and one non-production instance. The non-production instance is provided to you for development and testing.

You should strive to maintain both instances identical in terms of configuration and customizations, with all developments being done in the non-production instance first and then transferred to the production instance.

Occasionally, you will also want to clone your production instance onto the non-production instance to make sure they are in sync (Figure 8-12).

Update sets

Figure 8-12. Release developments from your non-production instance to your production instance

In ServiceNow changes are tracked and packaged in so-called Update sets (Figure 8-13). Developers export Update sets from the development instance and import them into the Production instance to apply all the developed changes at once.

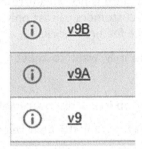

Figure 8-13. Multiple update sets may be associated with the same release

Testing and monitoring

In many software development organizations and at Al Jazeera it is common to have more than one non-production instance, with an instance dedicated just for testing.

Features that have been developed in the development instance are pushed to the test instance to be tested by end users. This allows developers to continue making developments in the development instances, without affecting functionality ready for testing in the test instance.

In Appendix A you will find more details about specific areas of the application that may benefit from additional testing and monitoring after deployment.

Release and deployment

Imposing the discipline of developing in a non-production instance first does not have to be associated with delayed releases in production. Facebook, probably the most heavily used software platform in the world, releases new developments to Facebook.com twice a day.

The keys to frequent and stable releases are:

- Release in small chunks. Don't wait long before you release; try to always break down projects and features in a series of small, and thus relatively safe, releases.

- Involve your stakeholders. Even though your developers may be confident of the features developed, you want your customers to test and confirm they are indeed as they wanted before you release.

This is of paramount importance in managing expectations because it will give your stakeholders a sense of control over their working environment in ServiceNow, but also in the event that bugs show up they will be much more understanding because when they tested they could not detect them.

Please note that user testing here is not meant to be an alternative to developer testing; you should ask customers to test only once developers are confident from their side that the features work.

Finally, after the release you may want to meet with stakeholders again in order to:

1. get their feedback on issues discovered after release;

2. prioritize developments for the next release.

For your convenience, Appendix A also lists checklists to help you assess the complexity of your customizations and remind you of steps to take before and after release.

Tweet-ready takeaways

- If ServiceNow HI support helps troubleshoot and fix your SN change, then it's a configuration. Otherwise, it's a customization.

- It is easier to mold ServiceNow to run as suits your circumstances than to coerce your organization as suits OOB. This is why you customize.

- Eat your own dog food and track all issues and enhancement requests for your ServiceNow instance in the instance itself.

- "Ordinary people should be able to create meaningful applications for their organizations"—Fred Luddy

- Those who invest labor in making something consider it much more valuable than if it were done by others. Employ stakeholders.

Confidentiality

How to control access on a need-to-know basis without hindering cross-team collaboration

When on-boarding new teams and people to ServiceNow one key issue that you will have to confront is that of confidentiality. Who sees what will be a key question of every new team bringing their daily work life to ServiceNow.

In ServiceNow every user with the ITIL role can search, view, and modify any ticket in the system. First-time users of ServiceNow unaccustomed to such openings will find it discomforting.

Before ServiceNow, they were used to controlling the visibility of their communications and issues in mailboxes shared only with their close-knit team. Now that their work to-dos, their messages with customers and partners (and their spelling mistakes) are open to browsing scrutiny by anyone in the organization (with an ITIL role) can be discomforting.

Even if you have the leverage to impose ServiceNow, or if some teams are already used to publicly searchable tickets, you need to consider confidentiality more seriously as you bring more people and teams on-board. The more teams you bring, and the more you expect them to use ServiceNow, the more confidentiality will be important. Not acknowledging this may subtly hinder the adoption of ServiceNow.

In other cases, there will be articulate reasons as to why expanded access to ticket information is not acceptable. The reasons can be that the tickets handle confidential user information (such as the personal security number) or other technical details that could be leaked to outsiders.

© Gabriele Kahlout 2017

G. Kahlout, *Spinning Up ServiceNow*, DOI 10.1007/978-1-4842-2571-4_9

If you decide that you want to have confidentiality in ServiceNow, how should you do it? Do you just make all tickets assigned to HR visible only to HR? What about the other teams? And cross-team collaboration? And outsiders?

This chapter provides you with two solutions for your confidentiality requirements:

1. Domain separation: Rigidly separates tickets, users, and configuration

2. Access Control (ACL) rules: Enables teams to flexibly extend or restrict access to their tickets on a ticket-by-ticket basis

Scope of data protection

So what data exactly are we trying to protect? In ServiceNow, data can be essentially be categorized as:

1. tickets data, emails, and attachments;

2. users profile data;

3. other records for assets and equipment.

Arguably only tickets data and attachments are exposed in ServiceNow, whereas access to assets, contracts and other types of records in ServiceNow are more tightly controlled and require users to be granted specific access roles. For this, the focus of the confidentiality model here proposed is to protect access to tickets data, emails, and attachments.

As for Users data, it too is exposed to everyone with an ITIL role in ServiceNow; but the same user information is also available to everyone in the organization in the global address book (see Figure 9-1), and so it would not be a breach if it is also available in ServiceNow.

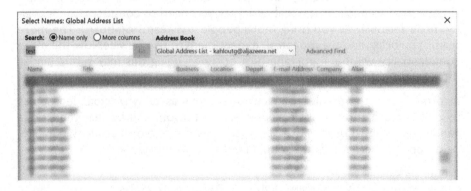

Figure 9-1. Global address book in Outlook can show all user profiles in your organization

You can, however, restrict what user information is available in ServiceNow by selecting what data is imported in ServiceNow from your directory server and, within ServiceNow, make certain fields only visible to certain groups. For example, you could make visible who is checked as a VIP in ServiceNow (see Figure 9-2) only to the service desk (see Chapter 3).

Figure 9-2. How the incident caller field changes for VIP users

Ticket data

For each ticket in ServiceNow, there are several layers of information that you may want to protect from access by people unrelated to the ticket:

- User-visible communication: Those are the messages of the caller and the user-visible replies she got on the ticket. They may sometimes contain sensitive details about the customer, or of things described in the reported issue.

- File attachments: The file attachments made to a ticket either by the caller or by people from the resolver team. Attachments can include screenshots that reveal sensitive information.

- Internal notes: The technical details and internal work notes about a ticket typed in by members of the resolver team and not shared with the customer because of their internal nature

- Ticket headers: The high-level details about a ticket that don't reveal the content of the ticket but give an indication about its status (see Figure 9-3). Ticket headers can be:
  - ticket number, caller and location;
  - status, assignment group, and assigned-to person;
  - timestamp of the ticket creation, and last update;
  - short description, category, and priority.

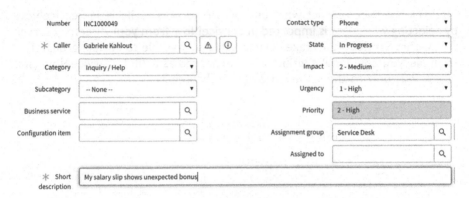

Figure 9-3. Without getting into details of the issue, header fields give information about the ticket and its status

Protection from ServiceNow

ServiceNow as a company will also have access to all of your data, hosting it on its own infrastructure. In fact, there is in ServiceNow a special access which ServiceNow HI support can use to log with administrative privilege into any instance; this special access is called "maint".

Going on the cloud, you trust ServiceNow not to eavesdrop on your data.

For this, Al Jazeera is among the ServiceNow customers that are not on the ServiceNow cloud, self-hosting their instances. But even self-hosting is not enough; so long as the instance is publicly accessible on the Internet, ServiceNow could access it also. The instance needs to be accessible only through VPN for maximum security.

ServiceNow also makes it possible to encrypt data, but if both the encrypted data and the keys to decrypt are with ServiceNow, they could again access this data.

ServiceNow's Edge Encryption also allows you to encrypt some data fields and host the keys to decrypt this data in your corporate network so that, although the data is hosted by ServiceNow, it would not be able to decrypt it without the keys hosted on your infrastructure.

Not all fields can be encrypted, however, and together with several limitations[1] and complexities Edge Encryption may be virtually impractical.

---

[1]https://docs.servicenow.com/bundle/helsinki-servicenow-platform/page/administer/edge-encryption/concept/c_EdgeEncryptionLimitations.html

Domain separation

Domain separation in ServiceNow, also known as multi-tenancy, lets you co-host many independent ServiceNow environments in the same instance. The concept is very similar to virtual servers co-hosted in isolation but in the same physical server, and goes beyond data protection.

Such separation is intended for Managed Service Providers (MSP), who could then have a completely separate environment for each of their clients, all in the same instance (see Figure 9-4).

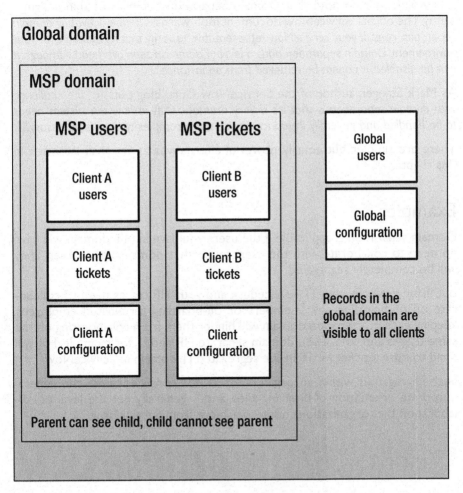

Figure 9-4. Domain separation in ServiceNow nests data and configuration

Under Domain Separation, the MSP starts with one ServiceNow environment, with all users in it. This is called the "global domain." The MSP can then create new sub-domains under the global domain, and assign users to each sub-domain. This way, the people in the sub-domain will only be able to see the tickets and data in their domain and not the ones in other sub-domains or in the parent domain. It will also be possible to customize forms and workflows in the sub-domain to be different from those in other domains.

Users in a parent domain (typically the support teams of the Service Provider) and ServiceNow administrators will have access to all data, in all sub-domains.

It is worthwhile to note that Domain Separation complicates things significantly. The official ServiceNow documentation warns: "*Before activating domain separation, consult your ServiceNow representative to verify that it is suitable for your environment. Domain separation adds a level of administration overhead. Although it can be disabled, it cannot be removed from an instance.*"[2]

As Mark Stanger, author of the ServiceNow Guru blog puts it: "*the challenge with domain separation is that it's a very dramatic shift in how the system needs to be handled and generally introduces much more complexity than is necessary.*"[3]

There are simpler but equally powerful alternatives as we shall later see in this chapter.

Examples

Domain separation is applicable if the users you have in one domain will have no need to collaborate with the users in another domain, whatsoever. They will be completely segregated.

But if, for example, your IT servicedesk and your HR teams need to collaborate on on-boarding new members or off-boarding terminated employees, keeping each in a separate domain will hinder them from collaborating on the same tickets and data. If you domain separate HR and IT, for example, HR will need to raise a ticket for IT in the segregated IT domain in ServiceNow.

Such segregation within an organization is not consistent with the general corporate orientation of breaking silos, and is generally not the level of collaboration that organizations hope to achieve from ServiceNow.

---

[2]https://docs.servicenow.com/bundle/helsinki-servicenow-platform/page/
administer/company-and-domain-separation/concept/domain-separation.html
[3]The challenge with domain separation is that it's a very dramatic shift in how the system
needs to be handled and generally introduces much more complexity than is necessary.

For example, ServiceNow quotes Kevin Barnard from GE Capital describing their ServiceNow implementation as: *"By teaming with the business, we've changed the way that people think about IT. There's no 'us and them'—we're all playing on the same side."*[4]

Domain separation puts everyone on a separate side, providing rigid splits of data and users that are normally not suitable for collaborating divisions of the same organization, but may be suitable for co-hosting multiple independent organizations under the same instance.

Domain separation could be suitable to segregate "legal cases" in the legal department, for example. It can be assumed that lawyers and staff in the legal department will work in isolation on most of their tickets, need strict separation and control of the data and can treat other users from within the organization as external users with limited access (until they sign a Non-disclosure agreement)!

But if you can avoid it, do. Even for legal, there many simpler solutions that can keep their data completely separate and confidential, without the complexity and, as ServiceNow called it, "level of administration overhead."

At Al Jazeera, for example, we do not use domain separation and have built new types of tickets for the legal department, with custom access roles. So only users from the legal department can see and work on legal cases in ServiceNow.

Other support teams at Al Jazeera use the standard Incident tickets in ServiceNow, and a lot more often collaborate and re-assign tickets across teams. They are also reassured of the confidentiality of their tickets, which they can control from within the ticket, as described below.

Access on a need-to-know basis

Besides the rigid option of Domain separation, you can customize ServiceNow to control access to tickets much more tightly, while also maintaining the flexibility needed to collaborate with other teams and users.

Access on a need-to-know basis means that only the people that need the access are granted such access by those that already have it, and is regarded as one of the tightest security mechanisms, making it difficult to leak information and browsing of sensitive data.

---

[4]https://www.servicenow.com/content/dam/servicenow/documents/case-studies/cs-ge-capital.pdf

This need-to-know access model can be implemented in ServiceNow by restricting access to tickets to only the people that need to collaborate on them and letting them extend it to others as they deem necessary on a ticket-by-ticket basis. More precisely, there would be three levels of access to a ticket (see Figure 9-5):

1. Read-only access to the ticket's basic headers available to all ITIL users

2. Full-access to the ticket granted only to members of the ticket's assignment group or those listed in the work notes lists

3. The caller and those listed in the ticket's watch list can download and add file attachments, as well as participate in the customer-visible comments.

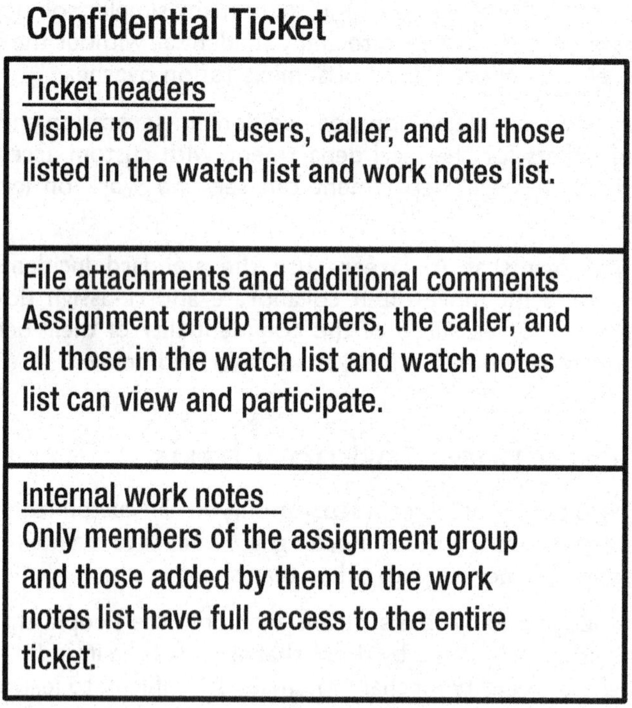

Confidential Ticket

Ticket headers
Visible to all ITIL users, caller, and all those listed in the watch list and work notes list.

File attachments and additional comments
Assignment group members, the caller, and all those in the watch list and watch notes list can view and participate.

Internal work notes
Only members of the assignment group and those added by them to the work notes list have full access to the entire ticket.

Figure 9-5. Different sections of the ticket are accessible to different groups of people

Put more simply, people in the assignment group of a ticket have full access to the ticket, and they can extend the same access to other people by adding them to the work notes list.

Adding people to the ticket's watchlist enables them to participate in the user communication of the ticket without seeing the internal messages.

In this way, confidentiality is tightly but flexibly controlled for every ticket, providing maximum flexibility to extend access to all the people that need it to collaborate on the ticket.

Variations

When proposing the need-to-know confidentiality model, questions may be raised about what access the servicedesk has. They may claim that they need to know more about every ticket.

As described above, the servicedesk and every ITIL user can preview all of a ticket's basic details so that they can report on the status of tickets to inquiring callers, reach the team to whom the ticket is assigned, or report to management.

Because of the specialized nature of tickets assigned to different teams, the servicedesk would rarely be able to support enquiring callers about the ticket, even if they had full access to the ticket. Otherwise, they would not have escalated the ticket to another team in the first place. So it is assumed that restricted access to the basic ticket headers is sufficient even for the central servicedesk.

At CERN[5] they have also proposed an interesting twist to this model by allowing service desk and other people that do not have access to view the comments on a ticket. They can, however, add a comment to the ticket that they themselves will not be able to see after submitting.

This should enable the servicedesk, for example, to leave a message on a confidential ticket by another team, without being able to view what else has been said on the ticket.

Sister teams

If you examine the actual patterns of collaboration, you will find that certain teams always collaborate more amongst each other than with any other team. Those teams are usually within the same department and share common resources, for example, network and IT system teams working closely together on maintaining the back end IT infrastructure, or various ERP teams working together on HR and finance issues.

---

[5]Z. Toteva, et al. "Service management at CERN with Service-Now," International Conference on Computing in High Energy and Nuclear Physics, 2012

Call these collaborating teams "sister teams" as in sister companies. An extension to the need-to-know model that enables more collaboration between sister teams would grant members of sister teams not only access to all tickets assigned to their team, but also to those assigned to their sister teams (Figure 9-6).

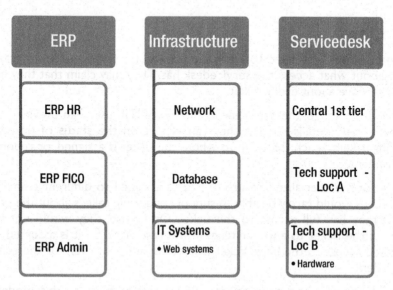

Figure 9-6. Sister teams tend to have a lot in common, and are much more likely to share secrets, or tickets

Confidential checkbox

So far the need-to-know model assumed confidentiality for all tickets. That is, every ticket in ServiceNow is elevated to confidential status and is by default only accessible to those that need to collaborate on the ticket. But if this is not necessary, you could also make confidentiality optional.

If tickets confidentiality is not so critical in your organization, you may make confidentiality optional with a checkbox in each ticket so that only when the checkbox is checked does the need-to-know confidential model apply.

When unchecked, the default access model in ServiceNow applies (that is, the ticket is public to all ITIL users).

Confidential scenarios

Below is a walk-through of real-world example tickets that illustrate the dynamics of a confidential ticket.

Personal ERP issue

1. Omayma, a member of staff, calls the servicedesk about an issue with her ERP details. She is forwarded to discuss the matter with the dedicated ERP support team.

2. Dina, dedicated to ERP support, logs an incident for Omayma's issue and assigns the ticket to the ERP HR team that specializes in such issues.

   At this point, Omayma (the caller) receives a copy of her incident by email. Logging in, she can also see the user-visible side of the ticket, while the ERP HR team has full access of the ticket.

   But, also, other sister ERP teams have access to the ticket, if it comes their way, while the Servicedesk and other ITIL teams can only see basic details about the ticket.

3. Saud of the ERP HR team fixes the issue and notifies Omayma about the solution of her issue.

4. Omayma receives the notification about her issue but, upon checking, she still has the issue and so she calls the Servicedesk again. The Servicedesk looks up her ticket and forwards her back to the ERP team.

5. This time, Sara from the ERP team receives the call from the Servicedesk and, although she is not from the ERP HR team, she has access to the ticket since she belongs to an ERP team, the sister of ERP HR.

6. Upon reviewing the issue with Omayma on the call and reviewing the feedback Saud left on the call, she attempts to troubleshoot the issue with Omayma on the phone. Lo and behold, they manage to fix the issue now.

7. For future reference, Sara writes a note about the issue and solution in the ticket and Saud is notified.

In this scenario, the Servicedesk received the call and forwarded the call to the specialist section, which in turn solved the issue.

For new tickets received via email, the ticket will not be confidential until it is assigned to a group. If you want all tickets to be confidential from the start, you need to ensure that every new ticket is either automatically assigned to a specific team based on certain criteria (refer to Chapter 4 for email-based assignment), or that it's by default assigned to a central Servicedesk team that then reroutes the ticket to the appropriate team.

Information security work

Consider a within-IT ticket opened for investigation by the Security team. The workflow would be something like this:

1. Barbarossa, from the Internet Security team, identifies a potential threat and logs a ticket for it under his name. He sets himself as the caller and assigns the ticket to his team.

    At this point, only his team has details of the ticket, while other ITIL users can merely find out that there is an open ticket logged for Security.

2. After internal discussion, Security decides to request changes to the network firewall and apply a security patch to desktop computers.

    So Barbarossa opens two new tickets (change requests), one for the network team and another for technical support citing "security concerns" as the motivation for the changes.

3. When opening the tickets for the network team and for technical support, Barbarossa made sure to be added to the work notes of the ticket, and so gained full access to the tickets. He had access over all three tickets opened about the issue, while each team had default access only to their ticket.

Note how Security is not expected to reassign its tickets to other teams. It instead should request action from other teams in new, dedicated tickets, and disclose as little as necessary about potential threats or compromises.

Confidential vs. Out-of-box

Out of the Box in ServiceNow, all ITIL users have full access to all tickets. Here is how (Table 9-1) the need-to-know access model described above (without sister team or service desk twists) differs from the defaults in ServiceNow.

Table 9-1. Who sees what in Out-of-box configuration versus need-to-know model

Acccess to ticket data

	Assignment group members	Other ITIL users	Caller	Other people
Ticket headers				
Out-of-box	Full access	Full access	Limited access	Can view some fields if added to watch list, or the ticket was opened by you
Need-to-know	Full access	Limited access	Limited access	Limited access
File attachments				
Out-of-box	Full access	Access only if in the work notes list	Full access	View-only access is added to watch list
Need-to-know	Full access	Full access only if added to work notes list	Full access	Full access only if added to watch list
User comments				
Out-of-box	Full access	Full access	Full access	No access*
Need-to-know	Full access	Access only if added to work notes list (or watch list)	Full access	Full access only if added to watch list
Work notes				
Out-of-box	Full access	Full access	No access	No access (must have ITIL)
Need-to-know	Full access	Access only if added to work notes list	No access	No access

It is important to note that once a valid ServiceNow user is for example forwarded an email chain about the ticket, they will be able to update the ticket by replying to the email even though they cannot do the same from the ticket. The same applies for ServiceNow Connect (see Chapter 10). With ServiceNow Connect you can do things to the ticket that you couldn't through the standard web interface (e.g., add attachments).

When changing your access control rules, it's important that you also consider how those rules apply, or can be circumvented, via email or ServiceNow Connect.

Arguments against confidentiality

As said before, the servicedesk may resent the limitations of confidentiality and request special access to all tickets. Other arguments may also be raised against confidentiality, such as those listed below.

"It's unnatural and complicates things"

Access on a need-to-know basis is consistent with what teams are used to already. When receiving a user inquiry, teams normally discuss it internally with their email group only and don't expect others to have access to the conversation, unless someone already with access shares it.

Further, with the reassurance that the information exchanged is only accessible by the people you see listed in the ticket, people are more likely to engage in personalized and detailed conversations. This should lead to better outcomes.

"Confidentiality discourages collaboration"

It is very unlikely that a person from the Network team finds on his own accord a ticket from the ERP team in ServiceNow, and proposes a solution to it. Most collaboration happens between related sister teams and upon invitation from those with access.

"It's still possible to have a data breach"

Just like a trusted person with access could still leak emails to outsiders, so it can be with ServiceNow tickets. But at least ServiceNow will log who shared access with whom.

"When reassigning to another team, they can see all previous conversations"

When reassigning tickets, once-confidential communication is now shared with the new assignment group. In practice, however, it's rare for a ticket to be reassigned to a group with whom the previous information needs to be hidden. When this is not desired, a new ticket should be opened with only the details necessary to share with the new team.

Tweet-ready takeaways

- Domain Separation in ServiceNow complicates things significantly and cements silos.

- Access on a need-to-know basis means that only the people that need the access are granted such access by those that already have it.

- You can use Access control rules in ServiceNow to implement a need-to-know access model to tickets that is both tight and flexible.

- Security shouldn't reassign its tickets to other teams. It should request action in new dedicated tickets disclosing as little as necessary.

Fluid collaboration

How to track internal collaboration in ServiceNow and reduce email traffic

From the first day that you introduce a service desk analyst to logging a ticket in ServiceNow, you will be asked about how to add entire email groups to receive updates on a ticket. In fact at Al Jazeera 47% of all emails received by ServiceNow in 2015 had at least another email address copied in other than the desk's.

Email groups are a common artifact of collaboration in corporate environments with almost every team in the organization having an email group for its members. There are normally more email groups than sections in the official organizational chart.

When an issue gets reported it is very common for one or more email groups to be copied in the CC. How do you want ServiceNow to deal with those CC recipients?

This chapter addresses various internal collaboration issues that typically bubble up only once ServiceNow is actively used in the organization. Read outside that context, some of the discussed issues and proposed solutions may seem unnecessarily complicated.

© Gabriele Kahlout 2017

G. Kahlout, *Spinning Up ServiceNow*, DOI 10.1007/978-1-4842-2571-4_10

We will consider both conventional solutions implemented by many ServiceNow customers as well as ServiceNow Connect, a new instant messaging interface that posts directly to the ticket and uses push notifications for alerts.

We will not be talking about Visual task boards as those offer a solution for collaboration at the queue level, while the collaboration discussed in this chapter is at the single ticket level.

In this chapter:

1. Groups in the CC: Copying email groups in the CC is a long-held corporate tradition. I tried and failed to undo it.

2. Customer-visible vs. internal: Not all messages about a ticket should go to the caller; what about back-end collaboration?

3. ServiceNow Connect: ServiceNow's Slack-like alternative to email.

4. Tracked emails: Email groups and the CC can work with ServiceNow.

Back story

When we launched ServiceNow at Al Jazeera I tried to counter the common tendency to copy entire groups in the CC reasoning that we should reduce the number of "For Your Information" (FYI) emails and that anyone interested could be individually subscribed to follow up on the ticket.

I had a perfect rationale (I felt) but in the end I observed that rather than change their workflow by not copying in groups, people would just not open a ticket and send their request by email with all the groups they want in the CC.

In other instances those that used ServiceNow tickets kept complaining about the limitation of not being able to look up and add groups and it became a sore issue with ServiceNow.

I realized that it basically was not up to me to tell if people should copy a whole email group or not, so in the end we gave them what they wanted in ServiceNow.

Another issue hindering behind-the-curtain collaboration in ServiceNow was that ServiceNow by default does not send email notifications for work notes added to an incident ticket; it only sends notifications for the communication with the caller.

So unless you are using ServiceNow Connect and, if you want to notify another colleague about a ticket (asking a question perhaps) you could not rely on ServiceNow for it because it would not trigger any notification. Your colleague would see the work note only if she for some reason opened the ticket and read the work note there.

User vs. internal communication

The resolution of many tickets requires more than just communication with the caller. There will be internal approvals, consultations with tier 3 and vendors, reassignments from team to team, or hand-over notes between one shift and another. How do you keep track of it all?

ServiceNow incident tickets come built-in with a thread to track messages with the customer in a journal field called Additional comments as show in Figure 10-1. This comments thread works in a predictable fashion: every comment that is added is recorded in the ticket and a notification is sent to the caller of the ticket, the assignee, and other people and emails listed in the ticket's watch list. You do not receive an email notification for comments that you add.

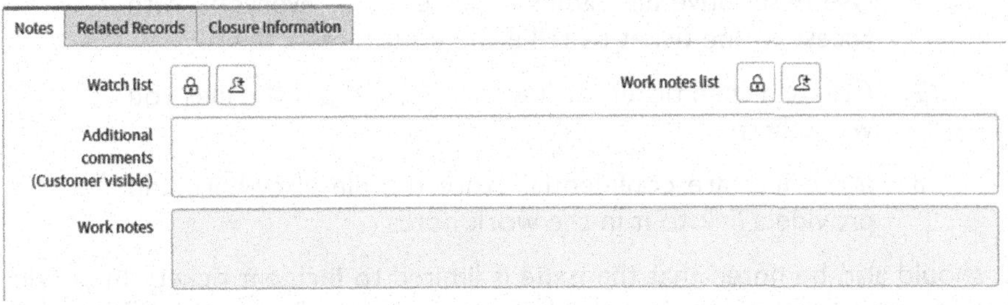

Figure 10-1. Watch list and Additional comments are for messages with the customer

Incident tickets also have a parallel thread for tracking work notes. Work notes are like comments but can only be viewed by users that have the ITIL role (so supposedly internal folks) but ServiceNow does not send out any notification for Work notes.

There is also a Work notes list in every Incident ticket but unlike the Watch list for comments there is no feature associated with it out of the box. It's left to you to decide what to do with it.

You can also mark the distinction between messages exchanged with the customer and internal ones more obviously by putting the related fields for each on a separate tab as shown in Figure 10-2.

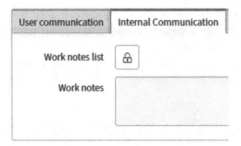

Figure 10-2. Internal and user-facing communication threads can be seperated in a tab each

Internal attachments

Sometimes internal conversations also involve internal attachments (such as detailed error logs) that would be irrelevant to the customer. So it may be requested to separate between user-visible attachments and internal ones.

This is however not supported in ServiceNow as there is only one attachments table, with attachments visible by default to everyone who has access to the ticket. Rather than twist this I recommended users to come up with creative workarounds such as:

1. Use descriptive file names so it's easy for everyone with access to the ticket to tell if the file interests them.

2. Create a child ticket for internal use and put the files you want there.

3. If the files are confidential, store the file elsewhere and provide a link to it in the work notes.

It should also be noted that the issue is limited to Incident tickets. In Service catalog requests the customer will have access to the Request and Requested item records, while support teams will have Catalog tasks assigned in which they can store their attachments separately from end users.

ServiceNow Connect

ServiceNow introduced a new option for collaborating on tickets dubbed Connect. ServiceNow Connect provides users with a chat-like interface with which they can update the work notes and comments of tickets (see Figure 10-3).

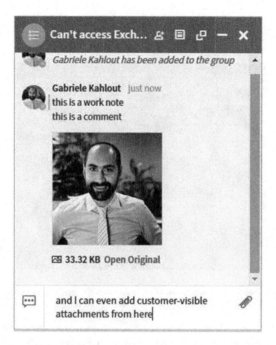

Figure 10-3. ServiceNow Connect offers a chat-like experience for updating tickets

Unlike the earlier legacy chat module in ServiceNow, Connect posts chat messages directly as full-fledged work notes (or customer-visible comments) on the ticket. It is exactly the same as if you updated the ticket through the regular ticket interface.

Together with a variety of in-app, desktop, and email notifications for ticket updates, Connect presents an interesting option for internal collaboration on tickets.

When there are new messages, the Connect Sidebar icon displays a balloon indicating the number of new messages received on tickets you are following. Expanding the Connect Sidebar (see Figure 10-4) you can preview those messages and reply through the chat interface or go to the updated record.

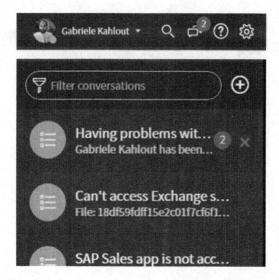

Figure 10-4. ServiceNow Connect sidebar is built into the ServiceNow application header

If a work note is posted on a message while you are away ServiceNow will alert you with an email such the one shown in Figure 10-5.

Figure 10-5. Email notification sent about messages received while you were not logged in to ServiceNow

Since users using a chat interface tend to write multiple shorter messages as opposed to one big update, the email notifications sent from Connect lump together a few minutes' worth of updates into one email instead of sending a notification for each message.

Connect notifications can also be pushed to users on a desktop computer through modern browsers support, and on the ServiceNow mobile app.

With the above features, ServiceNow Connect offers a viable and well-integrated option for internal collaboration on tickets and you may seriously consider it to reduce your organization's reliance on email.

Replacing email with ServiceNow Connect

While ServiceNow Connect is well-integrated with tickets and features a modern instant messaging interface end users and senior executives at your organization may not be interested in participating in such a communication channel.

Requiring everyone to log in to ServiceNow and use Connect to catch up on ticket updates and update them may not be acceptable.

As a softer start you may use ServiceNow Connect as your primary collaboration mechanism internally, bypassing the need to configure the work notes list in incident tickets and using Connect ticket conversations instead. Once your internal team is comfortable and accustomed to collaboration on Connect you may also introduce it for end users, replacing the default email notifications with those from Connect.

Connect also lets you control how long to wait before it sends an email notification for new messages added while the user was offline. You can gradually increase this time period to reduce the volume of emails triggered from ServiceNow.

Addressing Connect limitations

The default configuration of ServiceNow Connect may not be ready for enterprise-grade collaboration. Fortunately, most limitations can be address as discussed below:

Following a ticket

The ServiceNow Connect interface is still not the default in ServiceNow.

When a user assigns a ticket to himself, he is by default subscribed to receive comment updates to the ticket via email. But he will not receive Connect alerts because he would first need to click on the Follow button (see Figure 10-6).

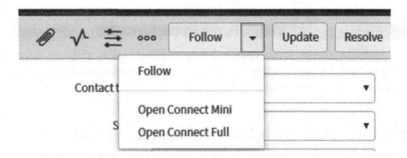

Figure 10-6. To receive a ticket's update on Connect you need to follow it first

If you are assigning the ticket to someone else as is so often the case, you cannot add that someone to receive Connect notifications, you have to follow the ticket yourself first. Then you can in Connect choose to add the people you want.

This may change in the future if Connect is adopted as the primary collaboration mechanism in ServiceNow.

Replies to Connect email notifications

Email replies to ServiceNow Connect email notifications create new incidents instead of updating the work notes.

You can however change this so that email replies are treated as work note updates. If you, set the Connect email notifications with the "INTERNAL:" prefix in the subject then email replies that contain it also will update the ticket for which the email has been triggered.

Groups and outsiders participation

The Connect interface only allows adding individuals with a user profile in ServiceNow; you cannot add external email addresses or entire groups.

Since Connect messages are integrated and posted as work notes you can have groups and external people participate in the conversation by adding them to the Work notes list or the Groups work notes list.

This way people already with access to Connect can participate via Connect, while entire groups and external collaborators can also chip in via internal email notifications. Because Connect messages are posted as work note, the communication should flow seamlessly amongst all users.

Other options

Even if you are going to use ServiceNow Connect you will still not be able to collaborate from ServiceNow with email groups or external vendors and email addresses.

For this you can implement the below described solutions either as an alternative to Connect altogether, or as complements.

Internal emails

When a ticket is assigned to you, you get an email notification of the assignment. What happens if you reply to this email questioning the assignment? Where will the reply go? To the caller of the incident!

You can however set it so that email replies to the assignment notifications are posted to the internal work notes instead, or set them to go to the assignment group's email address to keep things private.

More generally, you can configure an internal notification to be sent to the Work notes list subscribers whenever a new work note is posted, just like it is for comments and Watch list subscribers. This is a widely implemented solution in the ServiceNow community and is often featured in user manuals.[1]

For this to work smoothly and keep internal email replies from being posted to the customer, you need two things:

1. Prefix the subject line of your internal email notifications with recognizable prefixes such as "ASSIGNED TO YOU:" and prefix the email notification triggered to notify of new work notes with "INTERNAL:".

2. Configure ServiceNow to post to the Work notes any email reply that contains one of those internal prefixes.

So all email replies that contain "ASSIGNED TO YOU:", "UNASSIGNED:", "SLA DUE:", or "INTERNAL:" in the subject line should be posted as a Work note. All other email replies can continue to be posted as comments, as is by default.

In this way, your internal users and vendors can have their own email threads going on and automatically recorded in the work notes, while all other email replies that don't match the internal prefixes above continue to be posted as comments.

---

[1]http://huit.harvard.edu/files/huit/files/huit_inc_manual_v0-6.pdf

Copied in the CC

With the feature of automatically creating incidents from incoming emails some users expect that those they copy in the CC are added to the ticket's watch list automatically.

I personally resent this feature and as mentioned in Chapter 5 it can exacerbate the distribution of spam.[2]

Service desk stakeholders may however, argue that it speeds up tickets resolution by putting in the loop everyone involved from the beginning and that they otherwise would still have to add the people copied in emails but one by one manually.

When emailing the service desk with an issue that affects the entire team or a particular system, it is common for the caller to copy in the email a few extra people. The copied people tend to be:

- the caller's own team, so that they are also aware of the issue and don't report the same issue separately;

- the next person on shift, when the reporter of the incident expects to leave the shift before the resolution;

- the caller's line manager; this may be to leverage the political influence of the manager, to get her approval, or simply because the manager wants to stay tuned.

Apparently acknowledging this common feature request, ServiceNow's official wiki offers a useful script[3] for automatically adding email addresses copied into the CC of incoming emails to the watch list.

Groups watchlists

Just like you have watchlists for subscribing individuals to a ticket's updates you can have group watch lists to subscribe entire groups at once.

To be useful however the groups need to be in ServiceNow already and unless you are synching user groups with your directory server (see Chapter 3) this is unlikely to be the case.

Having a dedicated watch list for groups may also be useful for other reasons, as it allows ServiceNow to identify groups as more than just an email address, and know the members of the added groups. You could for example use group watch lists to control confidential access to tickets (see Chapter 9) at a group level.

---

[2]http://www.telegraph.co.uk/news/2016/11/14/nhs-it-blunder-sees -system-clogged-after-email-sent-to-12-millio/
[3]http://wiki.servicenow.com/index.php?title=Useful_Inbound_Email_Scripts

Tweet-ready takeaways

- There are normally more groups in the directory than there are organization units in the official organizational chart.

- Email replies that contain INTERNAL: and other internal prefixes in the subject line can be posted as Work notes.

Examples

Over 40 examples of ServiceNow customizations

This book focused on key aspects of ServiceNow as an enterprise collaboration tool considering it a real achievement if you managed for ServiceNow to blend in the daily collaboration routines of your organization. For this, Part II shed light on smooth and professional-looking communication with end users, while in Part III we also looked at internal collaboration behind the curtain and data confidentiality.

For your inspiration, this chapter will also give you a brief overview of over 40 customizations that may be relevant for your organization as well.

The customizations mentioned here are by no means exhaustive of what you may actually need in your organization as each is highly dependent on circumstances. Some customizations may even add unnecessary complication!

Unlike the recommendations discussed in earlier chapters, do not take any of the customizations briefly discussed here as a recommendation that you also implement it in your instance. Quite the opposite, only if the dynamics of your organization inevitably require you to make changes similar to those described here then consider this as a possible tried-and-tested solution.

Most of the screenshots and examples given refer to Incident tickets as Incident management is normally the first ITIL process implemented in ServiceNow and incidents end up being the most frequently used ticket type. Many of the customizations however can also been made to other ticket types such as Catalog tasks, Change Requests, and Problem tickets, with the required adaptations.

© Gabriele Kahlout 2017
G. Kahlout, *Spinning Up ServiceNow*, DOI 10.1007/978-1-4842-2571-4_11

For context, some features discussed in earlier chapters will also be repeated here with a brief description and a reference to the chapter in which it was fully discussed. Without further ado, let's get into it!

Search in ServiceNow

You may find the default search behavior in ServiceNow somewhat difficult; Here are a few customizations to lift the default limitations on search and make search easy again:

1. Contains search by default

One thing you will inevitably notice your ServiceNow administrator do when searching for something in ServiceNow is to type a * before the search keyword.

This is because ServiceNow will only search for records that start with your keywords but if you put a * in front of your search keyword, it will look for all records that contain the keyword, be it at the start, middle, or end. You can make the default search mode to be *contains* search so there is no need to type * as shown in Figure 11-1.

Location:	portacabin
Configuration item:	AJ Portacabin 1 AJ Portacabin 2

Figure 11-1. It is easier to fill forms in ServiceNow with contains search.

2. Personalized global search

The global search box in the top-right corner of every ServiceNow page (Figure 11-2) offers the quickest way to look things up in ServiceNow. But it shows search results from all the tickets in the instance, which if you are in a large organization, can be hundreds of thousands.

Most of the time however, you are looking for a ticket that you opened or for a ticket a colleague in your team referred you to, and are not interested in tickets logged on the other end of the world. So you will have to dig deeper and modify the search query to find what you were looking for.

Figure 11-2. The global search box in the top-right corner searches all records in ServiceNow.

You could however customize the default search results to be prefiltered for tickets assigned or opened by your team (Figure 11-3). That way, by default you get what you want most of the time from the first time you search, while for less frequent searches you can modify the search filters.

Conditions					
	Add Filter Condition	Add "OR" Clause			

	Assignment group ▼	is ▼	javascript:getAllMyGroups()	🔍	AND OR ✕
or	Opened by ▼	is ▼	javascript:getGroupMembers	🔍	✕
or	Email to ▼	contains ▼	javascript:gs.getUserID()	🔍	✕
or	Email to (internal) ▼	contains ▼	javascript:gs.getUserID()	🔍	✕
or	Opened by ▼	is ▼	javascript:gs.getUserID()	🔍	✕
or	Opened by ▼	is ▼	javascript:getGroupMembers	🔍	✕
or	Opened by ▼	is ▼	javascript:getGroupMembers	🔍	✕

Figure 11-3. The default filters for global search can be made more local or personalized.

Note, if you have implemented a tickets confidentiality solution (Chapter 9) in such a way that other teams cannot even see the presence of confidential tickets, then you may not need to add filters because ServiceNow will then by default not show you tickets that you do not have access to.

3. Color-coded ticket numbers

The state of a ticket is essentially one of three: Open, on hold, or closed.

To quickly identify the state of a ticket in a list without reading the state field, you can color-code the background of the number field with a color to denote each state (Figure 11-4).

A transparent background could mean that the ticket is open (either new or work in progress), amber that it is on hold, and green that it has been resolved (or closed).

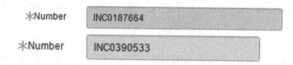

Figure 11-4. Green background color for the number field of a closed ticket, and amber for a ticket on hold.

4. Look up callers by staff ID

When receiving a phone call, the Servicedesk can ask callers for their staff ID and use it to immediately look them up directly in a new incident record (Figure 11-5). Once the caller is identified, the agent can preview recent tickets for the caller in ServiceNow or continue logging a new incident ticket.

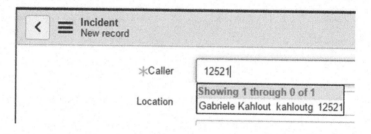

Figure 11-5. Asking callers for their staff ID is often much easier than spelling their full name.

Contextual help, dates and usability

Chapter 8 emphasized the importance of usability and convenience changes to encourage desirable behavior and increase user satisfaction, but also encourage usage of the system in the first place. Here are some usability tips.

5. Info messages with hyperlink

Once a ticket is updated in ServiceNow it can take a few steps to get back to it again!

For practical convenience, whenever a ticket is submitted or updated you could show an overhead info message confirming the change that just took place and providing a hyperlink back to the ticket (Figure 11-6).

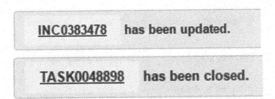

Figure 11-6. Information messages with hyperlinks that can take you back to the ticket or that you can use to copy the hyperlink to the ticket.

Such conveniences can be very useful for first-time users as well as advanced users operating under pressure.

6. International date format

Dates in ServiceNow are used to report on when a ticket was opened, last updated, or closed. Dates are also used in the Due date field if you set a deadline for a Task or Project.

ServiceNow allows each user to set their date format but as you can imagine most users will simply not do it. If you have users across the world, each will be used to a date format that is confusing to the other (dd-mm-yyyy in Europe and Asia and mm-dd-yyyy in America).

To elegantly circumvent this issue I recommend you set the default date format to the dd-mmm-yy format which is unequivocal on both sides of the Atlantic (Figure 11-7).

Opened   16-Feb-15 22:35

Figure 11-7. A ServiceNow opened field with the date in the dd-mmm-yy date format.

7. Rounded-up time fields

When scheduling the planned start and end dates of a change, you can go granular by the minute or round up to the earliest and latest 5-minutes interval as shown in Figure 11-8.

All changes' scheduled durations will be in multiples of 5 minutes which will be easier to remember and will fit more nicely in calendars. This is especially so if you display change requests on a shared global calendar.

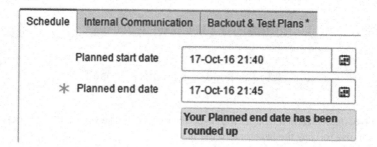

Figure II-8. Planned end date is conveniently rounded up so that the change duration is a multiple of 5 minutes.

8. Outlook global changes calendar

If you find ServiceNow's built-in Global changes calendar a bit clunky and you have your own Calendaring system (e.g., Outlook) you may create a sub-scribeable public calendar in Outlook that will show in real-time all scheduled Change requests in Outlook as shown in Figure II-9.

December 2014		Doha, QAT ▾	Today 30°C / 17°C		Search Change Management - Calendar (Ctrl... 🔎	
SUNDAY	MONDAY	TUESDAY	WEDNESDAY	THURSDAY	FRIDAY	SATURDAY
30 Nov	1 Dec	2	3	4	5	6
← From 16 Nov	CHG0036606 - AJE Corporate Network Infrastructure project for AJWT Phase 1; ServiceDesk					
	03:30 CHG00365...		07:25 CHG00365...	16:00 Test; Servi...	03:00 CHG00365...	19:13 CHG0364...
7	8	9	10	11	12	13
	CHG0036606 - AJE Corporate Network Infrastructure project for AJWT Phase 1; ServiceDesk					
12:00		CHG0036481 - Deploy ADFS Farm; ServiceDesk				18:00
14	15	16	17	18	19	20
CHG0036606 - AJE Corporate Network Infrastructure proj 18:30			19:00 CHG0036796 - Flushing 02-hv-cl01 Hyper-V cluster & Storage Luns + Backup Rem			
CHG0036604 - Develop Document Management System 1 17:18			00:00 CHG0036 7...	00:00 CHG0036 8...	20:00 CHG0036827 - Decommission Digita	

Figure II-9. Shared calendar in Outlook showing all changes planned in ServiceNow.

ServiceNow by default sends out calendar invites for Change requests to the person to whom the Change is assigned to. You can set it to also send the invite to your public calendar so that the changes are immediately visible on the shared calendar as well.

9. Read-only open details

By default, ServiceNow automatically sets the fields that capture who opened the ticket and the time when it was opened. Those fields are set as read-only so that they cannot be changed.

Some teams will argue that they need to log tickets with back dates, for example setting the opened date to when exactly the incident was experienced instead of when the incident ticket was logged. But if you enable ITIL users to set the opened date be ready to find tickets logged with future dates, unless you customize that the date cannot be set past the current time.

Also, the Caller field in ServiceNow is by default changeable by both ITIL users and the caller itself do you want to keep it this way?

10. Related records header

When setting the caller for a new Incident record, ServiceNow also allows the Servicedesk agent to quickly preview recent tickets for the caller to know if there is already a ticket for the caller's issue or if she had the same issue recently.

But the way the caller tickets are shown and the urgency on the phone may make it somewhat difficult to look through those recent tickets. You can customize what is shown as you deem suitable for example see the table header in Figure 11-10.

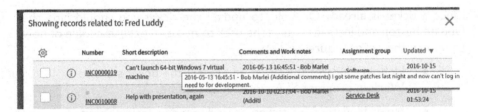

Figure 11-10. Adding the Comments and work notes field to the list view allows you to hover over the field and quickly preview the latest messages on the ticket.

Ticket state, priority and SLA

Chapter 5 on sending email notification described different templates for emails to send based on the ticket's state and the action required from the recipient, while Chapter 4 outlined how to deal with incoming emails, including email replies to ServiceNow notifications.

You may also customize the ServiceNow ticket front end to better control ticket state transitions, SLAs, and the setting of a ticket's priority as follows.

11. Buttons to change ticket state

A ticket's state is by default controlled through a drop-down field which ITIL users are expected to set as they update tickets. But there is also a Resolve button, which sets the ticket state to Resolved straightaway.

What will often happen however is that when updating a ticket many users may neglect setting the ticket state, for example, not changing it to or from On hold, although this is important for the calculations of the SLA and for the notification sent to the caller (see Chapter 5).

Just like with the Resolve button, you can have a Hold button that when clicked will save the ticket in the On hold status (Figure 11-11). If the button is clicked without writing a Comment to the caller you may also prompt the user to first type an explanation to the caller.

Figure 11-11. By clicking the Hold button the ticket will be saved in the On hold state.

Once a ticket is already On hold, to update the ticket you should hide the Update button and instead require the user to make an explicit choice of how to update the ticket (Figure 11-12):

- Unhold: Updates the ticket and resets the ticket state to Work in progress. SLA clocks may resume.

- Hold: Updates the ticket as still pending caller input. A message will be sent to the caller with the update, soliciting urgent update.

- Resolve: Updates the ticket as resolved.

Figure 11-12. Unhold updates the ticket and resets the state to Work in progress. Hold updates the ticket but keeps it on hold.

What if you want to cancel a ticket?

You could select the Cancel state and right-click on the ticket header and click on Save. Like Update, Save does not affect the state.

But you could also eliminate the need to fiddle with the state field and introduce a Cancel right-click menu item as shown below in Figure 11-13.

Figure 11-13. The context menu accessible by right-clicking a ticket header provides additional options to operate on a ticket.

12. Un-hold tickets automatically

When a ticket is put on hold it makes sense for the SLA to also be paused while awaiting customer updates.

But as soon as a new comment is received on the ticket via email or through the self-service portal the ticket should automatically be put back in the Work in progress state and the SLA clock should resume. Otherwise would defeat the purpose of the SLA.

13. Close on-hold tickets

It happens that sometimes tickets put On hold are ignored by the caller and never receive an update again. For this, you can set up ServiceNow to automatically close tickets on hold that have not received an update in more than seven days (or any number of days you deem appropriate).

If you introduce this behavior, remember to make it obvious to the users. When viewing a ticket currently on hold, show an information bar message informing that the ticket is on hold and after how many more days will it be automatically closed (Figure 11-14).

> Please note this incident will be archived automatically if no update takes place within 6 days.

✳ Number   INC0393472

Figure 11-14. Notice shown when viewing on-hold tickets, informing that the ticket will soon be automatically closed if not updated.

14. Replies to closed tickets

By default, email replies to a closed ticket do not reopen it and thus don't restart the SLA.

To make sure the replies do not go unnoticed you can list those tickets in a special list on the home page of your Servicedesk who will then decide whether to re-open the tickets or just note the provided feedback. For details about handling email replies to closed ticket notifications, see Chapter 4.

15. Re-opened incidents

What should happen when a ticket is intentionally re-opened by the caller? You may set tickets to be automatically re-assigned to the Servicedesk team to troubleshoot.

If the ticket was previously assigned to a person in another team chances are that she may not be available on shift to pick up the ticket again, and so the ticket may unnecessarily go neglected for a while. How you configure the re-open workflow depends on the nature of your support organization and the urgency of tickets.

16. Priority and SLA setting

By default in ServiceNow users do not set a ticket's priority directly but the priority is computed based on low-medium-high settings of Impact and Urgency fields, while the caller can set the Urgency of the ticket.

At Al Jazeera we have tied SLAs to the ticket's priority and also made it more straightforward to set the priority. The default priority of a received incident via email or self-service is Medium (P2) with an SLA of 10 hours as shown below in Figure 11-15.

ITIL users can freely change the priority of the ticket but to do so they also need to write an internal work note in the ticket explaining their reasoning. Also, callers are not given information about the ticket priority or urgency.

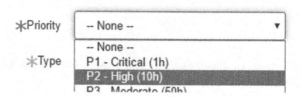

Figure 11-15. You can make it mandatory for ITIL users to explicitly set the ticket's priority when logging the ticket.

17. SLA reminders gauge

ServiceNow comes pre-configured to send two email notifications for SLAs:

1. One email is sent to the assignee of the ticket to warn when the SLA on the ticket is about to breach.

2. If the SLA is breached however, the notification is sent to the manager of the assignee.

And if the ticket is not assigned to anyone, no email notification is sent out.

Especially at the beginning, users and management will be excited about those notifications and may require the configuration of more SLA alerts (e.g., alert when the ticket SLA reaches 50%), send an email notification to the whole team, etc.

In addition or alternatively to SLA notifications you can create a home page gauge that shows the number of open tickets with active SLAs due to breach within 10 hours or already breached.

As shown in Figure 11-16 this will give the team a lot more visibility about tickets before they breach and hopefully enable them to re-negotiate priorities and eventually meet more SLAs.

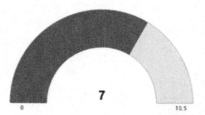

Figure 11-16. Dial to monitor the number of team tickets with running SLAs soon to breach.

As with other ServiceNow gauges clicking on the gauge will list for you the tickets in question as shown in Figure 11-17 so you can drill in and take action.

Figure 11-17. Clicking on the SLA gauge you can drill into the tickets.

Alternatively you could show an SLA progress bar as in Figure 11-18.

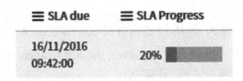

Figure 11-18. SLA progress bar

There is also a home page in ServiceNow dedicated to SLA reports (shown in Figure 11-19) if you want to get a more detailed view of the SLAs for your teams as well as all other SLAs tracked in the instance.

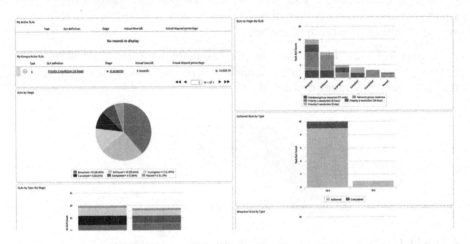

Figure 11-19. Out-of-box home page dedicated to SLAs.

Assignment, participation and hand-over notes

It's possible to automate the assignment of tickets in ServiceNow based on the caller of the Incident, the location, or the email address that it was sent to.

Here is how it works, together with other customizations meant to encourage internal collaboration best practices.

18. Assignment based on email address or location

You can automatically route incoming emails directly to certain assignment groups based on the email address that they were sent to.

But if the support request was sent to the generic support email address, you could assign the ticket based on the sender's location.

The workflow to assign an incoming new incident could be the following:

- If the incident ticket was auto-created from email then assign the ticket to the team registered to be assigned tickets sent to the addressed email, if any.

- If the location of the user is known or another location for the incident has been set then the ticket is automatically assigned to the team registered to be assigned tickets for that location.

- If the ticket could not be assigned to any group it should be assigned to a specific team you set as a catchall fallback option.

For more on setting user locations based on their OU in Active Directory, refer to Chapter 3.

19. Assignment based on Configuration item

Since ServiceNow is not just for the Servicedesk many tickets ought to be assigned to other teams.

One mechanism to determine to whom the ticket should be assigned is by setting the Support group field in Configuration items (CIs).

Based on the selected Configuration item of the ticket the Assignment group is automatically populated with the Support group of the selected CI, if any is set (see Figure 11-20).

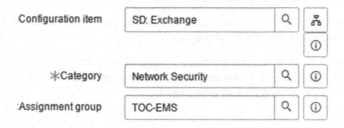

Figure 11-20. The assignment group can be automatically set based on the Configuration Item selected.

20. Discard unregistered emails

Because it is easy to redirect emails to your ServiceNow instance some teams may set up automated redirects to ServiceNow without agreeing on who should handle those income tickets and how they should be handled. Many of those may even be automated alerts from systems that they manage.

Our ServiceNow instance at Al Jazeera regularly receives tons of internal emails such as these.

By default ServiceNow would process any incoming email and since unrelated to any existing ticket, open a new ticket for each new email. This will flood the Servicedesk who puzzled and frustrated will not know what to do with the incoming alerts or who to assign them to.

You can avoid this problem by requiring that ServiceNow only process emails sent to recipients it is configured to receive emails from and for which you have configured an assignment group.

This way, even when someone redirects alerts to be automatically sent to ServiceNow nothing will happen on the tickets side until you explicitly config-ure ServiceNow to accept those emails and auto- assign them to a particular team.

21. Re-assignment pop-up

When tickets are assigned between teams or even team members, teams and people on the receiving end of the ticket may be confused as to why the ticket has been dumped onto them and may re-assign it back or ignore it for a while.

Especially when tickets are escalated to tier 3 teams, the receiver will want to see that the Servicedesk agent assigning a ticket made an effort to trouble-shoot the issue first and collected some basic details that will help in the resolution (steps to reproduce, screenshots, MAC address, etc.).

In order to encourage such hand-over notes when reassigning a ticket, you can show a pop-up (Figure 11-21) every time a ticket is set to be reassigned and no internal work note has been typed.

At this point the agent will be reminded about the importance of leaving a note or two to the receiving colleagues.

Typing a work note does not need to be mandatory as it may sometimes be obvious why the ticket is being assigned. The pop-up as a reminder should be enough and conducive to good practice.

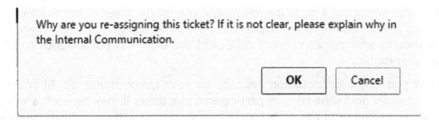

Why are you re-assigning this ticket? If it is not clear, please explain why in the Internal Communication.

OK   Cancel

Figure 11-21. Pop-up shown when a ticket is re-assigned to another person or team without leaving a work note.

22. Closing unassigned tickets

It can happen that for one reason or another, many tickets are closed without a name set in the Assigned to field.

If you want to report on the number of tickets assigned to each team member, you can make the Assigned to field mandatory when closing the ticket or just show a pop-up prompting the ITIL user closing the ticket to set the Assigned to field, as shown in Figure 11-22.

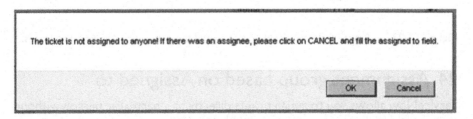

The ticket is not assigned to anyone! If there was an assignee, please click on CANCEL and fill the assigned to field.

OK   Cancel

Figure 11-22. Pop-up prompt shown to ITIL users closing a ticket that is not assigned to anyone.

23. Track participation

When you first introduce ServiceNow in your organization people will wonder which metrics will be used to measure teams' and individuals' performance. Should management report on the number of tickets assigned to individuals and teams, the number of tickets closed, opened, or what?

Some teams may also not be used to the concept of assigning ownership for the ticket to an individual person and may ask about the ability to count the participation of more than one person in a ticket.

In Private tasks created from the Visual task board ServiceNow now offers the ability to set additional assignees (Figure 11-23). You may customize and introduce similar behavior to incident tickets or keep it to one primary assignee per ticket and instead track participations from others as described below.

You may introduce a participation metric that keeps track of the number of tickets that an individual participated in. So in addition to the standard reporting metrics you can also report on tickets the user was not assigned to but collaborated in.

How you define participation depends on your circumstance. At Al Jazeera we consider someone to have participated in a ticket if they have left a work note or comment in the ticket, encouraging communication and making sure the contribution is actually felt and received by those working on the ticket.

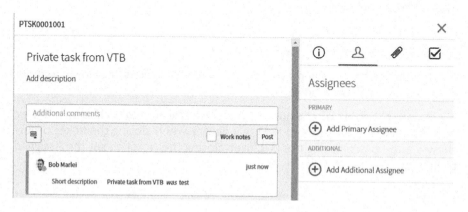

Figure 11-23. In Private tasks ServiceNow introduced the concept of Additional assignees.

24. Assignment group based on Assigned to

ServiceNow allows you to assign tickets directly to a particular person without assigning the ticket to a group (Figure 11-24). This may not fit the process by which other teams handle their collective workloads and may lead to disputes or to some tickets simply going unnoticed for a while.

If this is an issue for you, make setting the Assignment group mandatory once the Assigned to is set.

More conveniently, you can have the Assignment group of the ticket be automatically populated with the assignee's primary group (see Primary Group feature below, under Users and LDAP settings).

Priority	1 - Critical
Assignment group		Q
Assigned to	Bow Ruggeri	Q

Figure 11-24. Tickets in ServiceNow can be assigned to an individual without also assigning it to the group that she belongs to.

25. Parent assignment groups

If you have a lot of teams in ServiceNow, chances are that you will introduce some hierarchy to nest related groups (Figure 11-25). This will help new Servicedesk agents navigate through groups based on some logical grouping of teams (e.g., by location, or by function).

The problem with nested groups is that tickets could now be assigned to parent groups, and go unnoticed for a while because all teams are focused on the tickets assigned to their team and have enough.

Ideally, they would consider the parent group their team and also pick up tickets from there, but if that is impractical you could have ServiceNow forbid the assignment to parent groups. So tickets could only be assigned to child groups but not their parents.

Figure 11-25. Related teams can be nested under Container groups for ease of navigation.

Also refer to Chapter 3 for granting consistent access rights through parent groups so that access rights automatically cascade to the groups under them.

26. User communication and internal tabs

As discussed in Chapter 11, for every ticket ServiceNow tracks two communication threads: One for the messages exchanged with the end user, and one for those exchanged internally between resolver teams and perhaps vendors.

For compactness ServiceNow has recently combined the two threads and text boxes into one single text box and added a checkbox to determine if what you type should be posted as a comment or as an internal work note.

If users find this confusing and start mixing up messages by posting internal notes to end users, you can split the two threads into two separate tabs as shown below in Figure 11-26.

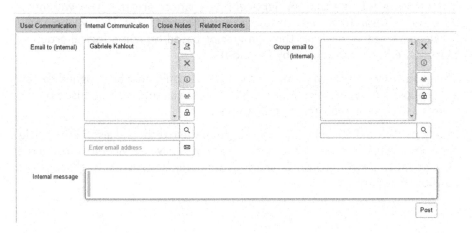

Figure 11-26. Separating the Comments user communication thread from the internal Work notes thread into two distinct tabs.

26. Vendor ticket number

Some issues require consultation with external vendors and partners such as with ServiceNow HI.

As in the case with getting support from ServiceNow if you cannot get vendors to use your instance you may still need a way to indicate that the ticket in your instance is related to a ticket somewhere else. This is to be used for hand-over or future reference.

You could invite people to simply note vendor ticket numbers in the work notes, or add a Vendor ticket number field dedicated to storing such information.

For letting some suppliers and partners collaborate on tickets directly in your instance, see Chapter 3 for vendors access and Chapter 9 for controlling tickets confidentiality.

Users and LDAP settings

Chapter 3 described how to import users into ServiceNow from your directory servers, optimize availability, tighten security, and manage access. Here are a few more situation-specific customizations that you may also find relevant:

27. Primary group

In the assignment section earlier, I described how you can have the assignment group of a ticket automatically populated once the Assigned to field is set based on the assignee's primary group.

For this to work, you need to add a Primary group field to each user profile in ServiceNow and have it automatically default to the smallest group the person is a member of, or set manually from the user profile.

When collecting approvals, you could take the group manager of the Primary group of the user to be the section head.

Finally, some ITIL users may be part of several teams that they work with, or supervise, on different days and may require seeing only a team's particular tickets queue on particular days.

You could build custom home pages for them, or have a home page that shows your primary group's tickets. With the latter, they can change their primary group and only see the tickets for the group they want.

28. Functional accounts

When we first went live with ServiceNow we had set up the Active Directory integration to sync user profiles with the Users OU in Active Directory.

Where all your user profiles reside in your directory depends on your specific setup but you may need to log tickets for functional accounts such as legal@your-company.com. These groups may be in a separate OU from your main users.

29. Email required for sync

In a dynamic organization user profiles may be in flux with new freelancers joining and leaving, and changing profile details. Your directory may also store temporary or phantom accounts used for testing or other purposes.

To ensure your users' details in ServiceNow are as clean as possible I recommend that you only import user profiles that have a registered email address, assuming every staff member has an email address. Otherwise if you log a ticket for callers that have no email address associated, they are not going to receive any email notifications about their ticket.

30. Unique user attributes

To ensure duplicate accounts are not created in ServiceNow or that ticket updates are sent to the wrong person, ensure that no two users have the same:

> Full name (a.k.a. display name)
>
> Email address
>
> User ID
>
> Staff ID

For uniquely identifying users and matching them between your directory servers and ServiceNow, it would be better if you rely on an immutable ID provided by your directory server for each user profile.

Microsoft's Active Directory assigns each user a unique identifier called ObjectSID (and there is also another globally unique identifier called object-GUID). Never changing, this field is the best to identify and sync users.

31. Location in tickets

Every ServiceNow ticket has a location field that is by default hidden from the incident form.

If your callers report incidents from different locations, or location is an important attribute of how you deal and route incidents then show the location field in incident forms, as in Figure 11-27.

Locations can be imported from your organization's directory servers together with user or department details. You can also define or add locations in ServiceNow.

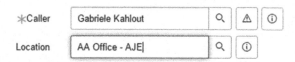

Figure 11-27. The default incident form in ServiceNow does not show a location field. But if you add the Location field, ServiceNow will conveniently prepopulate it for you based on the caller's location (if known).

32. Delete role

In ServiceNow access to delete records is constrained to those with the ITIL-admin role while to delete Assets you need the SAM access role.

You may however further restrict the deletion of records only allowing admins to do so, or those with a new CanDelete access role that you selectively grant to certain people only.

33. Access to add vendors

As with access to delete records, in ServiceNow people with the user_admin role can add, modify, or delete users or companies' records.

You may also want to have a new special role that only allows managing companies' records (used for tracking contracts and assets by vendors) but not users. This could then be safely used by your contracts administrators and asset custodians.

34. User details in preview window

For every Incident caller ServiceNow provides a convenience preview window to quickly see more details about the Caller (Figure 11-28).

Imagine the Servicedesk agent listening to the caller on the phone and glancing over the preview window on the screen and pick what user details you imagine she will want see in the preview window (the more fields you put, the more likely that she will not see them).

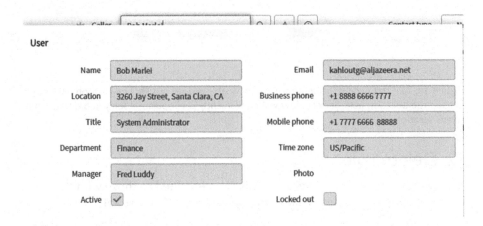

Figure 11-28. You can choose which user details are shown in the Caller preview window of Incident tickets.

The details you set to show in the preview window will be the same shown also in Request tickets for the Requester and wherever else user details are looked up.

If ServiceNow system administrators (or user_admins) occasionally need to see other fields as well such as those related to the LDAP integration then add those to the view but with security constraints that make them visible only to users with the admin or user_admin role. For more details about access roles see Chapter 3.

Request fulfillment

Chapter 6 talked about the end-to-end process of ordering something on ServiceNow. Here are some complementary customizations to help your fulfiller teams fulfill the incoming requests.

35. Request form and communication

When the Servicedesk (or another fulfillment team) is assigned a Catalog task they will see whom the request is for and the short description of the Task (Figure 11-29).

Number	TASK0010001		Approval	Not Yet Requested	▼
Assigned to		🔍	Priority	4 - Low	▼
Configuration item		🔍	State	Open	▼
Active	✓		Request item	RITM0010001	🔍 ⓘ
			Requested for	Gabriel Head	🔍 ⓘ

| Short description | Remote Access - Gabriel Head (REQ0041147) | | 🔍 |

Figure 11-29. Catalog task for a Request.

In order to view more details about what is requested, one would have to abandon the task and navigate to the Requested item (RITM) record. There you can see the form as it was submitted. The same goes for viewing the comments exchanged with the requester; You would have to navigate to the RITM or the Request (REQ) record.

Alternatively you could make those directly visible in the Catalog task under a Request Form tab and a User communication tab as show in Figures 11-30 and 11-31.

| ✳Short description | Remote Access – Gabriel Head (REQ004 |

Parents: REQ0041147   >   RITM0041871   >   TASK0107616

| User Communication | Internal Communication | Request Form |

Figure 11-30. In a Catalog task you can show the entire form submitted in a tab.

| Configuring Catalog Task form | | | | Cancel | Save |

Available		Selected	
Additional assignee list	▲	Request.Watch list	▲
Additional comments		Request.Additional comments	

Figure 11-31. Catalog tasks can be configured to show directly the Request's comments rather than have a separate User communication channel of its own. You can have the Request's comments conveniently shown in the User communication tab of the Catalog task.

36. Request tickets descriptions

When a new incident is received via email the subject line is by default set as the Incident's short description.

In the case of Requests submitted by filling an online form there is not a Subject field and thus the Short description is often composed from the name of the form submitted. For example, if I submit a request filling the Remote Access form the short description of the Request will be:

Remote Access for Gabriele Kahlout

Unless the workflow specifies otherwise the short description of the fulfillment Catalog task generated for the request could also be:

Remote Access – Gabriele Kahlout (REQ0041147)

This is all nice and clear for this request. But sometimes the request does not have a dedicated form, for example, for the installation of a special software and so the Short descriptions would be set as:

Other software for Gabriele Kahlout

Others – Gabriele Kahlout (REQ0041177)

Sifting through ticket lists (or emails) with generic descriptions such as those is not the best.

To get a more descriptive description you can let the person changing the Short description of a Task associated with the Request to also change the Request's description at once.

So in the above example the descriptions would be more descriptively described as follows:

Upgrade Balsamiq Mockups for Gabriele Kahlout

When you change a TASK, RITM, or REQ's short description you get a pop-up prompt (Figure 11-32) that asks you:

Did you want to rename the REQ and all of its child tickets?

- Yes, change them all.
- No, change just this TASK.

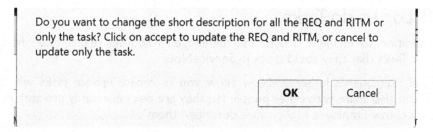

Do you want to change the short description for all the REQ and RITM or only the task? Click on accept to update the REQ and RITM, or cancel to update only the task.

OK   Cancel

Figure 11-32. Example pop-up displayed when changing the short description of a Catalog Task.

You could alternatively remediate the problem of generic descriptions by either adding a Request short description field in the forms so that the requester could fill it, or by seeking to create a Catalog form for each possibly requestable item.

But the more forms you show the user, the more difficult it will be for the requester to find the one needed. The same goes for fields in the form; the more I have to fill, the more daunting the task.

37. Wait for new ad-hoc Task

Sometimes a request will be more involving to fulfill than defined in the default Workflow.

For this you can give fulfillment teams the flexibility to list new ad-hoc Catalog tasks under the Request so that the Request is not automatically closed as soon as the Tasks generated by the Workflow are complete. The Workflow will also wait for all open Tasks associated with the Request.

You may make this more flexible by allowing any ticket (Catalog task or Change) to be associated with a Request, so that you do not have to create a new Task just to hold the Workflow if a ticket already exists.

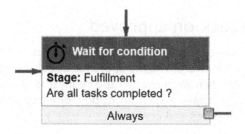

Figure 11-33. You can specify In the Workflow that governs Request fulfillment in your instance not to close the Request until all tasks associated with the request have also been closed.

38. Log to-do Tasks

In addition to Incident tickets and full-fledged Requests teams often have other Tasks that they could track in ServiceNow.

Visual task boards in ServiceNow allow you to create Private tasks which you can also share with other people (so they are not necessarily private). As ServiceNow Employee Molly Clark described them[1]:

"Private tasks are not really private (so maybe not the greatest name!). They can still be viewed and reported on like other tasks. They are just intended to be a very basic task to capture someone's other "work" that often doesn't have a particular requester, may not need to be assigned, probably doesn't need SLAs, etc, etc. This is often someone's general "to do" list."

Alternatively you can also use the familiar Catalog tasks as stand-alone Tasks that behave just like other Catalog tasks but without association to a Request or Workflow.

39. Reminder Task for return dates

Many requests are temporary, for example a temporary laptop that is required only for a day or a week. For such requests you can have ServiceNow create a new reminder Task for the Servicedesk to follow up on the return of the item, as shown in Figure 11-34.

Reminders for your Team				
⚙	Number	Opened	Short description	Messages
☐ ⓘ		13-Oct-16 12:57	RETIRE Laptop for Albara	

Figure 11-34. On the home page you can show a list of reminders due on the day for the team to remember and process.

40. No going back on approved

Once a Catalog request or a Change Request is approved the Workflow of the request will move forward. Yet, the approver could still go back and reject the Approval request again even though the request is already approved and in the fulfillment stage. Leaving such an option open to approvers can be a potential source of disputes and confusion.

---

[1] https://express.servicenow.com/support/forums/topic/ptsk-vs-task/

To avoid it, set approvals as final. Once an Approval request is approved the approval cannot be renegaded. The approver can still request to cancel or alter the request, but this will trigger the right set of actions and expectations.

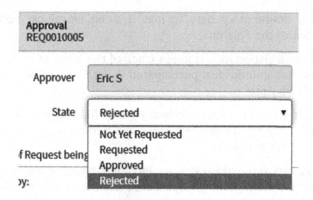

Figure 11-35. Even though a request may be approved and moved into fulfillment approvers could potentially go back and renegade their approval. This will trigger an email notification to the requester, but the workflow will have already passed the approval stage.

41. Consistent workflows

The Request Workflow applies to all received Requests in ServiceNow ensuring consistency for all Requests. However after the Request workflow, the Requested item workflow will kick-in and this can be different for each requestable item.

But chances are that there will be a lot of similarity between most, if not all of your items' approval and fulfillment Workflows.

As such, strive to re-use the same Workflows as much as possible to ensure a consistent user experience with Requests on the portal and so that bug fixes and improvements apply for all Requests.

42. Cannot reopen requests

Unlike for incidents if the user replies to a closed Request there will be no option to re-open the Request. You can however have a new Incident ticket linked to the Request.

Tweet-ready takeaways

- Customizations are highly dependent on circumstances. Some may even add unnecessary complication!

- The dd-mmm-yy date format is unequivocal on both sides of the Atlantic.

- A participation metric keeps track of the number of tickets that an individual participated in with a Comment or a Work note.

- Each user could have a Primary group field automatically defaulting to the smallest group the person is a member of, or set manually.

- You can automatically route incoming emails directly to certain assignment groups based on the email address that the emails were sent to.

- If you find ServiceNow's Global changes calendar clunky, you can get all change requests to show directly in a public calendar in Outlook.

ServiceNow jargon

Crash course on basic ServiceNow terminology

You have invested the time to read this book about ServiceNow, which I hope you found worthwhile.

Yet due to the non-technical nature of the book, you will still be unfamiliar with common ServiceNow terms that ServiceNow developers and administrators commonly use. Here is a quick explanation of frequently used ServiceNow terms, which should make communication with your ServiceNow technical colleagues much more fluid.

In this chapter:

- Scripting: What are Business rules, Client scripts and UI actions in simple terms.

- View: How you can show the same record differently, depending on who the user is.

- Deployment: How data and code are packaged from one instance to another.

- Reporting: How to control what is shown on users' home pages.

© Gabriele Kahlout 2017
G. Kahlout, *Spinning Up ServiceNow*, DOI 10.1007/978-1-4842-2571-4_12

Business rules, Client scripts and UI actions

Think of ServiceNow as a database of records (tickets, users, CMDB, etc.) with forms and pages to view, insert, and modify those records.

When a record is inserted or modified, Business Rules will run checks to ensure that the changes are consistent with how you want records in the database to be.

If a modification is found to violate any of your rules, it will be aborted and the records in the database will remain unchanged.

On top of aborting inconsistent changes to your database records, Business rules can also modify records based on user input, a query, or other related records.

For example, when the caller updates a closed ticket (either by replying to the closed email notification or through the Self-service form view of the ticket) you can have a Business rule that will also set a flag for the Servicedesk's attention. This is how the Noted feedback feature described in Chapter 5 is implemented.

Out-of-Box there is also a business rule that runs every time that a ticket is reassigned. The Business rule then increments the reassignment count field automatically (Figure 12-1).

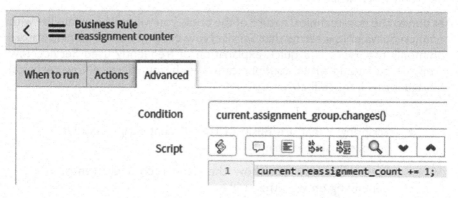

Figure 12-1. Out-of-box Business rule that increments the reassignment count field every time the assignment group changes.

The good thing about business rules is that they are applied consistently to records, regardless of whether the record modification is made through a form, list, email, or web service.

The down side is that the behavior of business rules is not transparent to users, and may easily overwrite or ignore their changes without them knowing it (see Figure 12-2). As discussed in Chapter 8 it is important that you make your application's behavior obvious to its users. So before you allow the introduction of a new business rule, check that:

- your new Business Rule displays a message that clarifies to the user the modification or action taken by the Business Rule (as shown in Figure 12-3);

- Avoid tampering with out-of-box Business rules as that can have undesired consequences and conflicts when you upgrade your instance.

> A business rule is a server-side script that runs when a record is displayed, inserted, deleted, or when a table is queried. Use business rules to automatically change values in form fields when the specified conditions are met. More Info

Figure 12-2. Info message shown when opening a Business rule in ServiceNow.

Incident reopened

Figure 12-3. Information message shown by an OOB BR when a ticket is reopened.

To discourage developers from inadvertently making your instance less maintainable, require explicit approval and justification before changes to out-of-box scripts are made. Otherwise developers should create new ones instead.

Even after you introduce a new Business rule, you may want to make its behavior predictable to the user even before she submits the form, and the BR applies. A typical example of this is the guidance messages dynamically shown as you choose a new password (see Figure 12-4) on a sign-up form.

Figure 12-4. Typical password field in a sign-up form shows immediate feedback to the user before she submits the form.

The server will never accept a weak password but the form uses immediate visible client-side indicators to inform the user up front, before she submits the form to the server.

The same can be done in ServiceNow with Client scripts (or another configuration) that runs transparently in front of the user.

Client scripts

Client Scripts are like business rules in that they intercept modifications made by a user on ServiceNow. The difference is that Client scripts intercept modifications to a form in real time, not to the record once it is submitted to the database.

So Client scripts run before business rules directly on the browser form opened by the user and based on her actions on the form, can be used to:

- Auto-fill fields on the form (Figures 12-5 and 12-6);

- Make fields on the form mandatory, locked, or hidden;

- Reject the setting of certain values and display an alert.

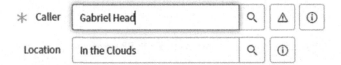

Figure 12-5. When you set or change the caller of an incident, the location field below is automatically updated with the user's location. This behavior is enabled by the OOB Client script "(BP) Set Location to User".

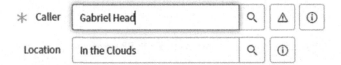

Figure 12-6. Auto-populating the Assignment group when the Assigned to field is set and making the Assignment group mandatory can be achieved with client scripts.

UI actions

A UI action is any button, link, or right-click context menu item in a form that allows the user to perform an action on the record.

What is special about UI Actions is that they can specify checks and behavior to run in the browser (Figure 12-7) and if all is fine, submit the record to the server (Figure 12-8).

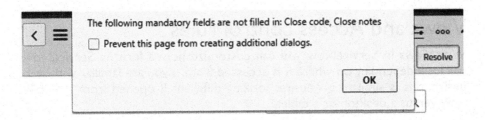

Figure 12-7. When clicking on the Resolve UI action, Close code and Close notes are visibly made mandatory, preventing submission of the record to the server until they are filled.

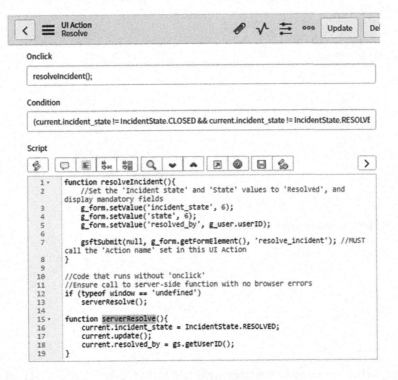

Figure 12-8. The Resolve UI action defines in the same script code to run on the client, as well as other code to run on the server.

To summarize, use Client scripts to interactively auto-fill fields in forms and Business rules for other settings that should apply to all records regardless of how the update is submitted (form, email, script). UI actions are buttons that can do things both on the form and on the server before BRs are run. Use them to make things easier for the user.

For more details about scripting in ServiceNow, check out ServiceNow's official documentation on scripting.[12]

Views and Access control rules

With Views in ServiceNow you can customize how a form in ServiceNow will look depending on where it is accessed from. If you are familiar with web design, this is similar to websites looking different if opened from a mobile view versus a desktop or a tablet.

For example, when an end user views an incident ticket she will see the Self-service view of the ticket (Figure 12-9); whereas when an ITIL user views the same ticket from his account he will see the default view for ITIL users. If the ticket is opened from a Visual task board the ticket will again look different (Figure 12-10).

Figure 12-9. Incident viewed in self-service view.

[1]http://wiki.servicenow.com/index.php?title=Differences_Among_Scripts
[2]https://docs.servicenow.com/bundle/istanbul-servicenow-platform/page/script/general-scripting/reference/r_17Scripts.html

Figure 12-10. Incident viewed from a Visual task board.

Creating views is not a mechanism to control who sees what; It is just a way to define the form layout (Figure 12-11) that is shown to different users. Users could still change the view or see all fields she has access to see on a ticket, by previewing the ticket history (Figure 12-12).

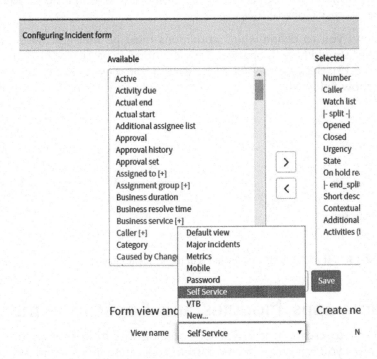

Figure 12-11. From the Form layout page you can select which fields are shown in each view.

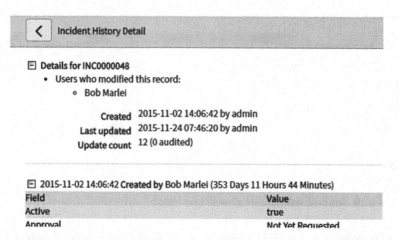

Figure 12-12. In the record's History detail log users can see all the fields that they have access to see.

To control who can see what or modify particular fields in a ticket you need to define Access Control Rules (ACLs).

ACL allows you to define which conditions must be met and which access role a user should have in order to view or modify a particular field in a form (Figure 12-13). Because of ACL rules even if you view ticket in a view that should show fields which you don't have access to you will not be able see them.

incident.caller_id	write	caller_id=javascript:gs.getUserID()^ORop...	record
incident.close_code	write	incident_state!=7^EQ	record
incident.close_notes	write	incident_state!=7^EQ	record

Figure 12-13. List of ACLs defined for fields in the incident table.

Custom apps, Modules, and Application menus

If you want to create a new type of ticket distinct from existing tickets in ServiceNow you can create a new custom application in ServiceNow.

A custom application in ServiceNow (Figure 12-14) allows you to create new ticket types and define who can access them (ACL), what Business rules to impose on them, email notifications triggered for them, etc.

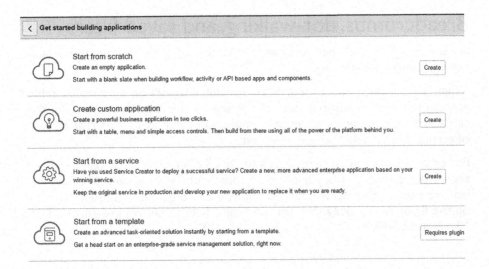

Figure 12-14. Options for creating new applications in ServiceNow.

Applications basically let you leverage all the ServiceNow ecosystem of email notifications, access control, forms, and scripts for a new process that you define.

Besides creating your own custom application, you could also browse, acquire, and install applications from ServiceNow third parties store.[3]

Each Application will have an Application menu section which is a section in the navigation menu.

You can, however, also create new Application menus that list links to multiple applications without all of them belonging to the same application. For example, the Self-service application menu in Figure 12-15 provides links to Incidents, the Knowledge base, and Visual task boards.

Figure 12-15. Self-Service is an Application menu. Menu items listed under it knowns as Modules.

---

[3]https://store.servicenow.com

Breadcrumbs, dot-walking, and saved filters

A very powerful tool that you have when searching and running reports in ServiceNow is dot-walking.

When previewing a list of records, or running a report on a particular table, you can select the fields that you want to see for the records in the table. You can also select the fields of records in another table as long as that table is reference from a field that you selected.

For example, say you want to view a list of all open tickets for callers whose accounts are inactive (they left the organization). There is no field called For inactive user in the incident ticket, but you could get the same information on the fly by dot-walking through the Caller field, as shown in Figures 12-16, 12-17, and 12-18.

Figure 12-16. To begin dot-walking, first select *Show Related Fields* from the drop-down menu.

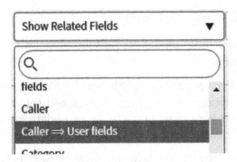

Figure 12-17. Select the new option that appears with an arrow (=>) below the reference field that you want to dot-walk.

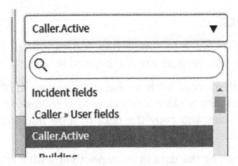

Figure 12-18. Finally in the dot-walk, select the field that you want.

The breadcrumb is the horizontal list of filters applied to the list of records that you are viewing. Filters on a list can be saved for future use as shown in Figure 12-19.

Figure 12-19. Filters in the breadcrumb can be saved so that you or colleagues can return to the same query again.

Update sets, Import sets, and Inbound actions

An Update set is ServiceNow's way to package changes for deployment from one instance to another.

Just like the Track Changes switch in Microsoft Word, only the changes that are made after the update set has been created and set will be tracked in the Update set. So developers must first create an update set and set it as their current Update set before they start making transferable changes.

When importing an Update set into an instance ServiceNow will compare the changes to the existing instance's code, show differences or conflicts, and prompt the administrator to either apply the changes or backtrack.

Importing data

Whereas Update sets were for importing code and configuration from one instance to another, Import sets are for importing data.

Data from external sources such as Excel sheets or LDAP servers is first imported into a temporary table in ServiceNow, an Import set. With the data in it you can apply rules and copy the data to a permanent record table that you specify.

The process of matching the data in an Import set with a table in ServiceNow is defined in a Transform map.

In a Transform map, you define which fields in the Import set should match which fields in your target ServiceNow table.

For example, if your Import set table contains User objects imported from your Active Directory, your transform map will map each User object field with the corresponding field in the User table (Figure 12-20).

≡ Source field	≡ Target field	≡ Coalesce
u_samaccountname	user_name	true
u_userprincipalname	email	false
u_l	location	false
u_source	source	false
u_givenname	first_name	false
u_sn	last_name	false
u_title	title	false

Figure 12-20. Default Transform map for matching user fields in Active Directory with user fields in ServiceNow.

In a transform map you also specify a *coalesce* field. This tells ServiceNow that while it imports the data from the Import set, it should check if there is already in the target table a record that has the same value in the coalesce field as the one that is about to be imported. If one is found, rather than create a new record ServiceNow will update the existing one instead.

A typical coalesce field for a user's Transform map is the user_name but it could also be the email address or the objectSID as discussed in Chapters 3 and 11.

Inbound email actions

Inbound Email actions are scripts (Figure 12-21) that define how to deal with incoming emails. Out of the box, they are configured to create and update incident tickets as was described in Chapter 5.

```
1    gs.include('validators');
2
3 ▾  if (current.getTableName() == "incident") {
4
5        var gr = current;
6
7        if (email.subject.toLowerCase().indexOf("please reopen") >= 0)
8            gr = new Incident().reopen(gr, email) || gr;
9
10       gr.comments = "reply from: " + email.origemail + "\n\n" + email.body_text;
11
12 ▾     if (gs.hasRole("itil")) {
13           if (email.body.assign != undefined)
14               gr.assigned_to = email.body.assign;
15
16           if (email.body.priority != undefined && isNumeric(email.body.priority))
17               gr.priority = email.body.priority;
18       }
19
20       gr.update();
21   }
```

Figure 12-21. Script of the inbound email action "Update Incident (BP)".

Task table, Sys_id and Dictionary overrides

Most of the tickets available in ServiceNow (Incident, Problem, Change Request, Catalog Task, etc.) all inherit fields and functionality from a parent Task table. This means that every Incident is by definition also a Task.

What this means for you is that if you want to run a report that lists both Problem tickets, Incidents, and Requests you can create a report on the Task table, as shown in Figure 12-22. It also means that if you want to have a feature, field, or common behavior on all your tickets you can define it at the Task level.

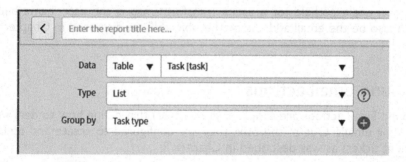

Figure 12-22. Reports can be created at the Task table level to report on multiple ticket types in the same report.

You could however override the property of a field inherited from the Task table by defining a dictionary override specific to a particular table. For example, you could have the Assigned to field labeled as Change owner in Change requests.

Every record in ServiceNow is assigned a unique 32-character ID: the sys_id.

It's like the number field but it is unique across all ServiceNow instances in the world. It looks like this: 9c573169c611228700193229fff72400

Home pages and Gauges

A home page in ServiceNow is a landing page that a user can be shown when they go to ServiceNow. By default there is a Self-service home page that is shown to end users while users with the ITIL role are shown the ITIL home page.

Each user can create and customize her own home page while administrators can also create, set, and control the home page of others.

A gauge is basically a widget or list that can be added to the home page. It can be created from a query or from a report.

Tweet-ready takeaways

- Think of ServiceNow as a database of records (tickets, users, CMDB, etc.) with forms and rules to view, insert, and modify those records.

- ServiceNow's Business rules run checks to ensure that changes are consistent with how you want records to be.

- Client scripts in Servicenow are useful for interactively auto-filling fields in forms.

- Creating Views in ServiceNow is not a mechanism to control who sees what; It is just a way to define a form's layout.

- ServiceNow dot-walking: You can select fields from another table as long as that table is referenced from a field that you selected.

Appendices

Your purpose is to make your audience see what you saw, hear what you heard, feel what you felt.

—Dale Carnegie

In this book I tried to organize and present topics typically overlooked by decision makers in charge of ServiceNow and the ITSM program at their organization.

I suggested that certain key elements in the way that you propose, implement, and expand ServiceNow at your organization can minimize the risks of failure and low users' adoption, and demonstrate early returns on the investment (ROI) in terms of customer satisfaction and an active user base. I proposed that having nurtured those early successes will give the firm foundations that you need before pursuing more advanced aspects of your ITSM initiative.

Throughout the book, I have tried to get into as few technical details as possible to illustrate the point being made; But if you are interested in more details, check out the following appendices.

Appendix A: Checks and Monitors

Appendix B: Access Requirements

Checks and Monitors

Checklists for before and after deployment

For your convenience, here you will find:

- Checklists to assess the risk of new customizations;
- Pre- and post-release checklists for new customizations;
- Gauges to monitor email sending and receiving activity;
- Charts to monitor and pinpoint performance issues.

Risk assessment

To determine the risk associated with a new change to ServiceNow consider the following questions:

- Is the change documented in ServiceNow's official online documentation (e.g., a property setting, enabling of a plugin, or a Useful script)?
- Does the new change modify code used to process incoming emails or outgoing notifications?
- Does the change involve server-side scripting, such as in a business rule or a script include?

© Gabriele Kahlout 2017
G. Kahlout, *Spinning Up ServiceNow*, DOI 10.1007/978-1-4842-2571-4_13

- Does the change modify how users are matched between your directory server and ServiceNow?

- Will the change affect all users or just those of a particular application (e.g., Asset Management)?

- Does the change mass update records at once (e.g., through a background script or scheduled job)?

- Will the change be deployed using update sets which can be rolled back or will it be performed in the instance?

The riskier the change the more careful you will want to be with testing and monitoring post-release.

You also want to make sure you have a fallback plan with stakeholders (e.g., temporarily stop emails redirected to ServiceNow) in case you end up needing some extra time.

Checks before deployment to Production

Before you commit your changes to the production instance it helps to set expectations with your stakeholders. Verify if:

- A ticket has been logged in ServiceNow describing the new feature or change;

- Stakeholders have been informed about the change and its potential impact on their use of ServiceNow;

- Training and documentation have been provided for how the new feature works (if necessary);

- The change has been made in a non-production environment similar to your production instance;

- There is testing evidence of the change working as expected;

- The change is consistent in behavior and usability with existing modules of the application;

- Possible side effects of the changes have been considered and tested (e.g., no duplicate emails are now generated).

Checks after deployment

After you deploy, and depending on what areas of the application were affected, you may want to test and monitor that:

- The new features work as expected in the live instance;

- All emails sent and received from ServiceNow after the change have a record attached to them and no error message;

- The number of emails sent for ticket updates after the change is consistent with your expectations;

- There are no new errors at the scheduled synchronization of users between your directory servers and ServiceNow;

- New tickets have been logged in successfully since the change and older ones have been updated with no issues.

Special checks

Depending on which modules you use in ServiceNow, you will normally want to inquire and carefully test changes that affect any of the following:

- Inbound email actions

- Email notifications

- LDAP sync settings

- Business rules

Inbound email actions

Inbound email actions are perhaps the most critical component of your ServiceNow application as it's responsible for processing incoming emails to your instance.

You want to avoid and minimize changes to such a central and impactful module in your application by making sure for example that your inbound email action scripts contain only code strictly related to the processing of emails and that it may be rarely changed.

If a change is made to an inbound email action script or a script include referenced from an inbound email action then you need to test and monitor the correct processing of incoming emails after the change is made. In particular, you should test that:

1. New incoming emails create new tickets correctly;

2. Replies to existing ticket emails update the correct ticket.

To be even surer and quickly uncover unexpected issues, you can also monitor emails processed since the changes were deployed. Monitor the following things in particular:

1. Error logs generated from the email processing scripts;

2. Incoming emails with an ignored status in ServiceNow or without an associated target record; That is, it didn't update any ticket (Figure A-1)

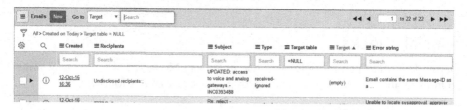

Figure A-1. Monitor incoming email logs for non-empty error messages and emails that updated no ticket.

Incoming emails monitor

You can create a gauge to monitor incoming emails that have not yet been matched with any ticket (Figure A-2).

Figure A-2. Create a report that you can pin to the home page to keep track of incoming email activity and possible issues.

If the number fluctuates it means that you are receiving emails, they are processed and matched with tickets, and the cycle repeats.

If instead the number remains stagnant you may have a problem processing emails (or you receive too few emails and they are processed very quickly).

In a busy instance, the number of unprocessed emails may not go down to zero as some emails are intentionally received and ignored. Clicking on the number you can preview the kind of emails that are unprocessed and confirm if there is an issue or not.

Outgoing emails monitor

Because it can happen that emails get stuck in ServiceNow and are not processed or that emails remain in the outbox queues but are not sent for hours add a gauge indicative of email activity to the home page of your Servicedesk (as in Figure A-3 or A-4).

Figure A-3. Gauge to keep track in real time of the number of emails in send-ready state.

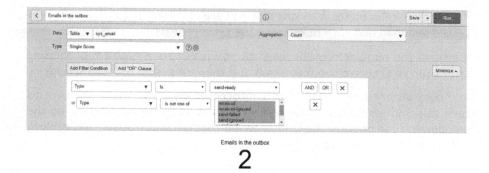

Emails in the outbox

2

Figure A-4. Counter to keep track in real time of the number of emails in send-ready state.

The gauges displays how many emails there are in send-ready state. If the number keeps fluctuating (going up and down), it means the instance is successfully generating new emails to send and sending them.

However if the number remains the same for a while or keeps going up only then you have a problem. There may be an issue sending emails through the email server (check connectivity with SMTP servers) or with email notifications not being generated (in case the number is always zero).

When setting the gauges you also want to track emails that are not of an unknown email types because that's likely to be an error state.

Email notifications

Email notifications settings in ServiceNow directly affect what your end users will receive or not receive from your instance. Tread carefully when changing, adding, or removing email notifications.

If you make changes to email notifications be sure to count and monitor how many emails are sent out about the same ticket at the same time. Changes to email notifications in ServiceNow can easily result in duplicate notifications being sent to the same people.

Your email notifications will also contain links, for example the link to preview the ticket in a web browser. Test those links after release as they may be broken or point to your non-development instance.

LDAP sync settings

Changes to your LDAP sync settings may result in the duplicate import of users from Active Directory or a failure to import new ones. After making changes, it is important to run a synchronization between the two and cross-check that:

1. The number of imported and updated users is consistent with your expectations;

2. There are no new errors in the LDAP logs.

Business rules

Business rules in ServiceNow basically define things that happen to the ticket on the server. For example assigning the ticket to a certain group based on the location of the caller.

Because the update happens after the user completes his action business rules can lead to unexpected behavior contrary to the user's will. For this reason you want to be careful with the introduction or edit of business rules and in particular check that:

1. The business rule doesn't silently overwrite a value the user had set on the form. If the value entered by the user is not what you want it to be, prevent the ticket from being submitted erroneously, or at least let the business rule inform the user.

   In some cases your business rule makes changes such as rounding time fields. In such case, let it also inform the user of the change.

2. the business rule doesn't conflict with other business rules that may also run on the same update.

Charts to measure slowness

If your users are complaining about slowness you can use a chart to crystallize who experienced slowness and when as well as compare the slowness to other time periods of the day or of the week (Figure A-5).

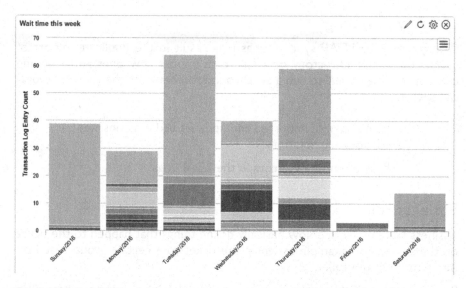

Figure A-5. Bar chart showing how many times users had to wait every day of the week.

Besides the satisfaction and sense of control that those charts provide you with they can also be very useful when reporting performance issues to ServiceNow.

In the chart settings you can control the sensitivity of wait time. In the settings shown below in Figure A-6 for example, we report on all user transactions in which the user had to wait more than 10 seconds. You can change the sensitivity of wait time as you see fit.

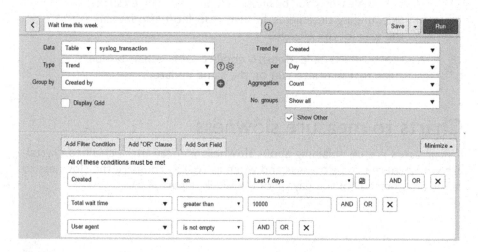

Figure A-6. The Trend chart counts how many times in the day users had to wait more than 10 seconds at once.

The colors staked in the bars of Figure A-5 represent the users that had to wait; if you click on each color you will be taken to the user transaction that took so long to execute as shown in Figure A-7.

		Created	URL	System ID	Total wait time ▼	Response time	Ser
		Search	Search	Search	Search	Search	Searc
☐	ⓘ	11-Oct-16 11:04	/api/now/ui/history?api=api	01-capri-08:app1	20,892	20,947	
☐	ⓘ	11-Oct-16 11:08	/api/now/connect/collaborators/8bf6a4673...	01-capri-08:app1	14,605	14,733	

All > Created on Last 7 days > Total wait time > 10000 > User agent is not empty > Created trend Tuesday > Created trend 2016 > Created by = kahloutg

Figure A-7. *From the chart you can drill and see details of the longest-running user transactions.*

The above chart in Figure A-5 is good to keep an eye on the application performance and quickly identify if performance seems to have suddenly worsened recently.

When you determine that slowness is indeed being experienced across the application you can check a few more charts like those in Figure A-8 to better understand the impact of the slowness and if there is any bottleneck.

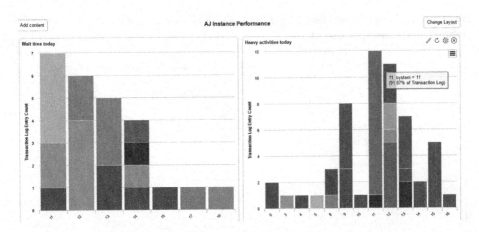

Figure A-8. *On a troubling day you can preview in which hours slowness was most experienced and compare if it coincided with long-running system transactions*

The chart above on the left shows users' wait time hour by hour during the day. The chart on the right shows all long-running transactions in ServiceNow also hour by hour during the day. Putting them next to each other you could identify if there are long-running system transactions that severely influenced user transactions wait time as well.

Finally on performance, day of the week comparisons of user wait times give you a good indication if performance is good on the day relative to other days of the week. But to get a better picture of your application performance in general you can extend the charts to a longer period of time as shown in Figures A-9 and A-10 below and see if things are relatively stable, improving, or worsening.

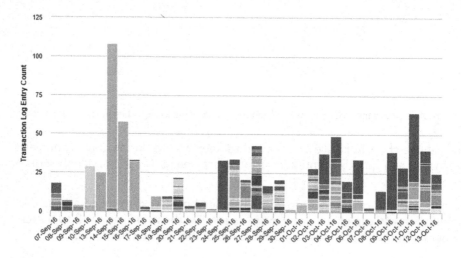

Figure A-9. Compare wait times over the past month to get a sense if performance is relatively stable, worsening, or improving.

Figure A-10. To compare performance over a longer period of time, create a Trend report trending by date.

Note that there are other charts and monitors mentioned in Chapters 3 and 11.

Access Requirements

Implementable bullet point requirements for LDAP and access control

A requirement documents a single need for a particular product or service.

—ServiceNow Wiki[1]

For your convenience, here you will find:

- a list of bullet points detailing LDAP integration requirements, based on Chapters 3 and 11;
- bullet point requirements to configure access on a need-to-know basis as discussed in Chapter 9.

Refer to Chapters 3, 9, and 11 for additional details or to better understand the rationale behind the proposed requirements.

---

[1]http://wiki.servicenow.com/index.php?title=Understand_the_Requirements

© Gabriele Kahlout 2017
G. Kahlout, *Spinning Up ServiceNow*, DOI 10.1007/978-1-4842-2571-4_14

Requirements format

ServiceNow distinguishes between functional requirements (what ServiceNow is expected to do) and corresponding technical constraints on how the requirement should be implemented.

With this understanding of requirements, here is a list of two-line functional requirements. If there is difficulty understanding any of them refer to the relevant chapter for additional details and context.

User access

For your Servicedesk to be able to effectively log and manage tickets in ServiceNow, everyone in your organization will need to have a user profile in ServiceNow even if they will never log in.

Here are proposed requirements for your ServiceNow instance to import and sync user profiles from your organization's directory servers and to provide your support team members with adequate access.

Prerequisites

ServiceNow comes with built-in support for the integration with Active Directory servers and ServiceNow's official documentation provides a comprehensive walk-through of all the steps involved in a standard integration.[2] [3]

Nonetheless, the integration is still a fairly technical set-up and requires collaboration between your Active Directory administrators, Network team, and your ServiceNow administrator. You may also need ServiceNow's involvement. Your SN administrator will need support to:

1. Obtain from your Active Directory administrators the integration end points of the Active Directory server to enter in ServiceNow as shown in Figure B-1:

   a. The address of the Active Directory server that ServiceNow should connect to;

   b. The credentials of a read-only account in AD that can be used to connect external applications like ServiceNow;

   c. The top-level OU name that contains all user profiles to be synchronized with ServiceNow;

---

[2]https://docs.servicenow.com/bundle/istanbul-servicenow-platform/page/
integrate/ldap/concept/c_LDAPIntegrationSetup.html
[3]http://wiki.servicenow.com/index.php?title=LDAP_Integration_Setup

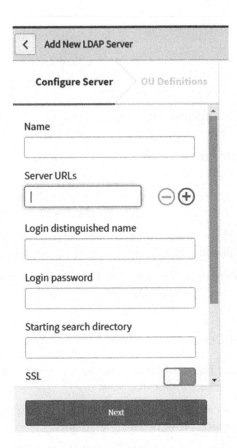

Figure B-1. LDAP server configuration step in the ITSM Guided Setup.

2. Get your Network team to enable ServiceNow servers to connect to the Active Directory servers of your organization. For this to happen, the Network team will have to whitelist traffic between ServiceNow and the Active Directory servers, possibly through a VPN tunnel (optional) or through an intermediary MID server.

If a VPN tunnel is to be established between ServiceNow's servers and your organization's directory server, you will also need to submit a request to ServiceNow's support on SN.HI.

User profiles

1. Create new user profiles in ServiceNow automatically for staff at your organization with details such as full name, email address, and staff ID number.

2. For each user profile in Active Directory there should be only one corresponding profile in ServiceNow.

3. Enable staff to log in to ServiceNow with their Active Directory credentials.

4. Update automatically existing user profiles in ServiceNow when their details are updated in Active Directory.

5. Enforce that no two users in ServiceNow can have the same email address, full name, user ID, or staff ID.

6. Do not import in ServiceNow accounts with an empty email address, name, or User ID.

Servicedesk access

1. Servicedesk team members should be able to view and update all tickets in ServiceNow.

2. Allow Servicedesk to add or remove members to their team in Service Now, or to other teams.

3. Adding or removing people from the Servicedesk group in Service Now should automatically grant or revoke associated access privileges.

Availability

1. Allow a ServiceNow administrator to log in to ServiceNow even when there is a problem with the LDAP integration.

2. Alert the Servicedesk and the ServiceNow administrator via email when an issue is detected with LDAP.

Security

1. Accounts disabled or expired in Active Directory should not be allowed to log in to ServiceNow, out of security concerns.

2. Changing a password in Active Directory should take effect in ServiceNow too; That is, no user should be able to log in to ServiceNow with the old password and the new password should work immediately in ServiceNow.

3. ServiceNow should only inquire Active Directory about the user profile fields desired to be in ServiceNow, not all available attributes in the Directory server.

4. Back-end communication between ServiceNow and directory servers should occur only through secure channels, to avoid malicious spoofing of passwords or users' data.

5. Restrict access to sensitive user details such as Staff ID.

Performance

1. Schedule the sync between ServiceNow and the Active Directory servers to occur once daily, outside peak hours.

2. Leverage performance optimization settings supported by ServiceNow and the Active Directory servers, such as Paging.

Vendors access

1. Develop a custom Vendor role and modify ServiceNow to allow assignment to teams with the vendor role while also forbidding them from viewing tickets not assigned to them.

   OR

2. Give vendors the ITIL role just like other teams but implement access on a need-to-know basis as recommended in Chapter 9. This way, it will be possible to assign tickets to them just like other teams but they will only be able to view and collaborate on tickets assigned to them or in which they are mentioned.

Other

Setting the user location based on LDAP setting depends on the Directory structure at the organization; refer to Chapter 11 for how it is at Al Jazeera.

You will also find a discussion about syncing groups and Single Sign-On in Chapter 3.

Access to data

Chapter 9 details a model to restrict access to ticket details on a need-to-know basis. Here is a bullet point summary of the proposed access model:

End-user accesss

1. At any one time, the caller and the people listed in the watchlist of the ticket can see and participate in the user-visible communication as well as download and manage file attachments.

2. Those already with access can extend or revoke same access by adding or removing people (or entire teams) from the watch list.

Full access

1. At any one time, only the team set as the assignment group of the ticket, "sister teams," and the people listed in the worknotes list have full access to the ticket.

2. Sister teams are the teams that have the same team as a parent (e.g., the Network team and the System team may have Infrastructure as a parent).

3. Those already with access can extend or revoke same access by adding or removing people (or entire teams) from the work notes lists.

4. If a ticket is not assigned to any group, it will not be confidential and all ITIL users will have full access to it until it is assigned to a team.

Others access

1. All ITIL users can preview basic ticket information such as its status and to whom it is assigned, but cannot alter it.

2. Access restrictions should apply uniformly to everybody, including ServiceNow administrators.

3. Impersonating a user should not grant the impersonator access to data she otherwise would not be able to view without the impersonation.

4. The same access constraints applied to a ticket should also apply to the body of emails and the file attachments related to the ticket.

For added flexibility, also implement group watchlists so that access can be extended to entire teams, rather than only on an individual basis.

So, there are now three levels of access to a ticket:

1. Read-only access to the ticket's basic headers, available to all ITIL users;

2. Full access to the ticket, granted only to members of the ticket's assignment group, sister teams, or those listed in the work notes lists;

3. The caller and those listed in the ticket's watch list can download and add file attachments, as well as participate in the user communication.

Index

© Gabriele Kahlout 2017

G. Kahlout, *Spinning Up ServiceNow*, DOI 10.1007/978-1-4842-2571-4

Get the eBook for only $4.99!

Why limit yourself?

Now you can take the weightless companion with you wherever you go and access your content on your PC, phone, tablet, or reader.

Since you've purchased this print book, we are happy to offer you the eBook for just $4.99.

Convenient and fully searchable, the PDF version enables you to easily find and copy code—or perform examples by quickly toggling between instructions and applications.

To learn more, go to http://www.apress.com/us/shop/companion or contact support@apress.com.

DATE DUE

GAYLORD		PRINTED IN U.S.A.

CPSIA information can be obtained
at www.ICGtesting.com
Printed in the USA
LVOW13s1940070518
576287LV00003B/153/P